SONSHIP

A JOURNEY INTO FATHER'S HEART

M. JAMES JORDAN

FATHERHEART
MINISTRIES
www.fatherheart.net

Fatherheart Media
www.fatherheart.net

© 2014

Sonship - by M. James Jordan
Third Edition published by Fatherheart Media 2014
First Published by Tree Of Life Media 2012

NOTE: THIS BOOK IS HAS THE SAME CONTENT AS THE PREVIOUS PUBLICATION
OF SONSHIP, THIS PUBLICATION ONLY HAS ANOTHER COVER IMAGE.

PO Box 1039, Taupo, New Zealand 3330
www.fatherheart.net

Printed in the USA/NZ

Cover Design by Tom Carroll

With special thanks to;
Wilson Sze, Erica Sze, Cathy Garratt,
Veikko Kosonen and Lloyd Ashton.

ISBN 13: 978-0-9941016-1-7

For other books, e-books, CD, DVD or MP3, visit www.fatherheart.net/shop Online international orders welcome. International shipping available.

To Jack and Dorothy Winter

CONTENTS

ACKNOWLEDGMENTS

I cannot do enough justice to the acknowledgement of Jack Winter as a major influence in my life. As a young Christian in Bible School, the Lord spoke to me in a clear voice telling me that He wanted me to be a 'Joshua' to this man Jack Winter. For the following twenty-five years Denise and I were firstly disciples to him but then we became respectively a spiritual son and daughter to him. As Joshua assimilated all that the Lord had commanded Moses, I tried to assimilate all that the Lord had imparted to Jack. Before Jack died, he laid his hands on me and prayed for the impartation of his mantle of anointing. I am trying to continue as Joshua did after Moses died, to enter a land over the river from the point of Jack's passing.

I want to acknowledge with great affection John and Sandy Randerson, Jan and Sandra Rijnbeek, my wife Denise and my children, Jack Winter (again) and a few others who continued to believe in me, held me up and carried me when I was unable to stand on my own.

I want to thank Stephen Hill for his hours of work without which this text would not have been possible. And thanks also to Wilson and Erica Sze for their encouragement and determination to see this get into print.

I want to thank the people of Fatherheart Ministries International for the companionship and encouragement along the way as we have explored the love of the Father together.

Lastly - I simply cannot find words - I don't think there are any - that say, "Thank You" sufficiently to our God and Father for His amazing plan and His ability to perform it in my life. He was with me before I was a Christian and since I became a Christian He has been faithful to me - unimpressed by my successes or failures. He just loves me.

PREFACE

In 1977, Jack Winter saw something in the midst of the myriad refractions and reflections of the Christianity of that time. It was a blazing flash of pure light. He saw into the very heart of God the Father. The consequences are still reverberating throughout Christendom to this day.

Jack and Dorothy Winter had lived an amazing adventure till that day. Filled with the Holy Spirit and faith they had journeyed into the unknown, abandoning the world and its cares, and living with a level of dedication to the Spirit and to the Word of God that is very rare. Before long, hundreds of others from around the world had joined them in what was called "Daystar Ministries". It was within this network of communities that Jack came across this opening into the Father's heart.

For the remaining twenty-five years of his life, Jack dedicated the extraordinary resources of his rich inner life and profound ministry experience exclusively to ministering the love of God. He had realized that this love was actually a substance, which could be imparted and which could heal the broken-hearted. Crisscrossing the globe, he flew well over one million miles, and spent from dawn until dark each day holding many thousands of people in his embrace, and seeing the wonderful healing of God. I was one of those people. Jack had seen the reality of God's fathering love – the culmination of New Testament revelation.

This book tells of my personal journey towards and into that light. Jack was a spiritual father for me and, before he died in August 2002, he laid his hands on me to receive his mantle. But even the blazing revelation of the Father's love that he had received was still only in part. There is always more. Here is the way I have found to the Father. His love being poured into my heart has led me from being simply a Christian into a life as a son of God. This has proven to be only the first step. There is always, excitingly, more. (James Jordan, Taupo 2012)

CHAPTER 1

The Father's Revealing

~

Over the past fifteen years, I have travelled around the world more than thirty-five times, speaking in countless conferences and churches, sharing on the revelation of the Father. I often feel that the Lord takes me around the world simply to tell people what has happened in my life. Someone once said to me, "James, you seem to think that the Father's love is the answer to every problem in humanity." Do I really believe that? I believe it with all my heart.

The further I go on in this revelation of the Father's love the more I am realizing that a complete renovation of Christianity is necessary. We have had a Christianity that is much too focused on what you have to do, and not on who God is and what He has done! Many of us carry the baggage of a presentation of the gospel that is false. We have been told what we must do from our initiative rather than what God has done from *His* initiative. We have been told that we have been blessed so that we will be a blessing to others. The simple fact is that we have been blessed because God loves us and because He just longs to bless us. We have been presented a gospel that tells us we must work for God – but I can tell you that this will, eventually, cause you to crash and burn. More and more Christians are opting out of this type of Christianity and getting off the treadmill of continually trying to please God and work for Him.

What Christianity is about is simply this: God loves you and He wants you to live in the continuous experiencing of Him loving you. That is the whole point of Christianity. Coming to this realisation brings us into rest and contentment and an inner peace that is so contagious that people will be impacted just by who we are. We are in a renovation, a reformation, and a restoration of Christianity that is, I believe, as significant as *the* Reformation itself.

KNOWING JESUS IS NOT THE SAME AS KNOWING THE FATHER

So much of the impression that I have gained of Christianity over the years is that it is all centred around Jesus. The Father is really only mentioned in passing. Indeed, the Father seems to be in the background compared to the person of Jesus. I believe this is because we have such a focus on the person of Jesus. We have the idea that if we know Jesus and have experienced Jesus then we automatically know the Father. John 14:7 is one of the verses which people get this misconception from, when Jesus said, "If you have seen Me you have seen the Father," but we need to remember that Jesus is *not* the Father and the Father is *not* Jesus. So Jesus was *not* saying, "I am the Father." He never said that knowing Him was the same as knowing the Father. He said that the Father was in Him doing the works. He spoke words that the Father told Him to say.

He said, "I only do what I see my Father doing" but He *never* said, "I *am* the Father."

Everything that we teach has to be based in Scripture. If we ever get a revelation that is not scripturally based then it is not a revelation from God. However, it must be said that walking according to the Scripture is not necessarily the same as walking with God. If you walk with God you will *automatically* walk according to Scripture. We walk in the Spirit, not in the Word, but the Spirit will never lead you in anything that the Word does not validate. The disciples never once read the New Testament. They wrote it! What was their source material? They walked by the Spirit and the Spirit gave them the Word to write.

I once read something by Andrew Murray which impacted me greatly and which leads into the purpose for writing this book. He wrote, *"What the Father's love was to Jesus, His love will be to us."* You see, the great shortcoming of our Christian experience is that even when we trust Christ we leave the Father out. *But Christ came to bring us to God the Father.* That was the whole point of His coming – to bring us to God the Father.

Andrew Murray then went on, *"His life of dependency on the Father was a life in the Father's love."* I really love that statement! The reason why He was able to depend on the Father was that He knew His Father loving Him totally and He could depend on that love. In everything that happened in His life He had total dependency on the Father. Then he makes the statement that I love the most, *"What the Father's love was to Jesus, His love will be to us."* What place in Jesus' life did the Father's love have? How important was the Father's love to Jesus? You would have to say that it was everything! He delighted to do the Father's will.

He lived in the experience and knowledge of the Father's love for Him. He was in the very bosom of the Father, eternally living there in the Father's heart. That was His place.

I believe that today we are seeing a revelation beginning to sweep around the world, a groundswell in the ocean that is going to rise up on the beaches like a tsunami and it is the restoration of the place of the Father in the Christian life.

Derek Prince, commenting on John 14:6, (where Jesus said, *"I am the way, the truth and the life. No one comes to the Father but by Me"*) made the following statement: *"This verse speaks about a pathway and a destination. Jesus is the way, the Father is the destination."* Then he made this observation, *"The problem with most of the church today is that we have become stuck on the way!"* We have become stuck on the Way! We have come to Jesus but we haven't gone on to intimate relationship with the Father. One of the reasons for this is that many of us have lacked intimate relationships with our earthly fathers and so, as we read verses like this, we just do not see it. We interpret our theology as being all about Jesus. I believe, however, that Jesus would have said, "It's not all about Me. It's all about My Father."

We are in a time when the foundation of our Christianity is moving from being a two-legged stool, so to speak, to being a three-legged stool. We have had a revelation of Jesus and a revelation of the Holy Spirit and we have based our Christianity on these two realities because revelation *is* reality to our hearts. Now, however, God is bringing to us a revelation of Himself as Father and, because God is love, it is an experience of love. It is based on a personal and intimate invasion of the love of the Father into our hearts. For some people this comes in a mighty rush, while for others it just dribbles in bit by bit. It doesn't really matter how it comes, as long as it comes. In fact, revelation often comes to us like the gradual dawning of a new day.

In laying the foundation of what the Father is to be in the Christian life, I want to quote from St. Augustine of Hippo who said, *"The whole of the Bible does nothing but tell of God's love. This is the message that supports and explains all the other messages."* Every Christian subject that you can possibly think of is an expression of the love of the Father. Indeed, *everything* in Christianity is about the love of the Father. Christianity without understanding and experiencing the love of the Father is a Christianity that is missing its foundation.

Something will be awry with our concept of what it means to be a Christian if we do not have the Father's love as the foundation. Even the cross is an expression of the love of the Father. The love of the Father is not an expression of the cross. For God so loved the world that He gave His only Son, and His dying on the cross was, in that sense, the greatest message of how much God loves us. It expresses what the love of God is really like. The whole point of Christianity is the love of the Father, and the cross removes everything that comes between us and that love so that we can come boldly to the throne of grace and climb right onto His knee, to know Him as our Father. Our Christianity will be very distorted if we do not understand that the love of the Father is the revelation that supports and explains all the other messages.

Augustine says further, *"If the written word of the Bible could be changed into a single word and become one single voice – this voice more powerful than the roaring of the sea would cry out, 'The Father loves you!'"*

You see, we do not know what we do not know! We do not know that we don't know the Father. We know the doctrine and we can even teach people about knowing God as Father without personally knowing Him as a father ourselves. A revelation changes our perspective so much that, without thinking about it, we automatically begin to address God as "Father!" We can know the Scriptures *about* the Father, and we can think that knowing the Scriptures is equal to knowing the Father Himself! We don't know that we don't know!

One of the major problems in Christianity today is the belief that if we know what the Bible says then we automatically have what it is talking about. This is a major misconception. As I teach on this I very often come across this misconception. It can be a particular problem for those, like myself, with an academic bent. For many years I thought that knowledge of the Scriptures was the same as having the reality of what the Scriptures are talking about. It led me into a totally false belief in where I stood with God, which was ultimately shattered by a personal failure. When that happened, I suddenly realized that all my knowledge did not change me one bit! I cried out to God for something that would change me.

We are living today in a time when God is revealing Himself as Father in a way that is unprecedented since the time of the apostles. No matter what you have known and experienced in the past, there is an unprecedented level of the Father's love still available. If we can open our hearts to it, He can transform our whole experience of Christianity into something far greater. Christianity really begins when we come to experience what Jesus died on the cross for us to receive – the Father's love!

Let me begin the story of how I came into this revelation. When

Denise and I came to the Lord in 1972, we came from outside of anything that was remotely Christian. We had no exposure whatsoever to Christianity. The nearest building to the house where I grew up was a little church up on the hill. I used to see people going there. Some of them were my school friends, but I had no idea why they would want to spend a beautiful Sunday morning in a church. I had no understanding at all. I had never even heard the term "born again."

When I was almost twenty-two years of age, I gave my life to the Lord. My salvation had been a monumental change in my life, because from boyhood onwards I had been an extremely lonely young person. We lived in a small country town and most of the time I didn't have anyone around to play with. The nearest boys of my age were at least three miles away, so after school and on most weekends I would roam by myself around the fields and farms beyond our house. Oftentimes after school I would be wandering on the range of hills nearby until darkness fell and then I would walk back home across the land, over the farm tracks, climbing the fences and gates. I knew it all very well, but I was very alone.

So when Jesus came into my life, into my extreme loneliness, it made a huge impact on me. Suddenly there was this Person coming into my heart who loved me, and I fell in love with Jesus because of this. My salvation was literally an experience of glorious technicolour. Never was the sky a brighter blue or the grass a fresher green.

BORN INTO REVIVAL

When I got saved, Denise and I started to go to a church that was in revival. Many Americans use the term "a revival" in the same way that we would use the term "an outreach" for a series of evangelistic meetings. But revival, as I have come to understand it, is when the presence and power of God is so strongly manifested that people experience it in a very tangible way. When a revival comes, it always has a significant effect on our experience of Christianity. A true revival is when God's presence shows up with extreme power. It is an overwhelming release of His presence in a particular place.

Amazing things happened in this church during that revival time. There was a young woman there who wanted to learn how to play the piano to accompany worship but she had never had a music lesson in her life. One day she sat down at the piano, one of the deacons prayed for her, and immediately she could play in any key that she chose. She could not play the piano apart from accompanying worship and she began to take music lessons some sixteen years later to discover what she had been doing all those years.

At times, people were actually seeing Jesus walk through the church, up and down the aisles and laying hands on people, just touching them as He walked past. Many people would have a corporate vision and would see exactly the same thing at the same time within the services. One of the elders would welcome visitors, then invite the Holy Spirit to come, and we would just go with what happened. For about five years there was no need for a pastor or leader in the meetings because the Holy Spirit was so powerfully evident. It was an extraordinary period of time. It placed a hunger in me to experience revival continually and since then I have had an expectation and hope that maybe it will happen again today. We cannot make it happen however. It is totally up to Him.

Looking back on that time I realize something else. When the Spirit of God was so powerfully manifested, I made a misguided assumption that the reason He was honouring our church with His presence was because the teaching was perfectly accurate. Many people throughout history and all over the world today are making the same misguided assumption. We assume that, if we get our interpretation and application of Scripture exactly right, then He will come and honour it with His manifest presence. That just isn't true! Actually, that very assumption is the basis of much dissension amongst Christians today. The reality is, however, that He doesn't come because the teaching is right, but His coming actually *corrects* the teaching. The Word is only really understood in His presence. The Bible was written in revival. Every person who wrote it was living in a personal and total revival. It is written about revival and it is only understood in revival.

So we were experiencing a tremendous sense of His presence, Sunday after Sunday, year after year, and people were coming from all around the world. Before long, the elders of the church decided to organize a conference. The only place in town big enough to hold the crowds was the local horseracing track, where there was a big grandstand, and many people attended to hear some of the best speakers in the world in that day. It was a huge blessing for us to be exposed to the ministry of some of these international speakers and the anointing that was in these meetings. However, working on the assumption that God was pouring out blessing because of the rightness of the teaching, I assimilated absolutely everything that was preached and taught. It never occurred to me to question that it could be anything other than absolute truth.

I remember there was one particular speaker at the conference, who preached a message that really impacted me and which

I totally accepted without questioning. He preached from the text where Jesus took Peter, James and John up to the Mount of Transfiguration. He talked about how Jesus was transfigured and how the figure of His being was changed and clothed in the glory of the Lord, and how they saw (at least to some level) Him revealed as He had been in eternity. In the midst of this they saw Moses and Elijah appear with Him. The Father spoke from the cloud, "*This is My Beloved Son. Listen to Him*" and the three disciples fell unconscious to the ground. After some time had passed they looked up and "*saw Jesus only.*" (KJV). Moses and Elijah had left and Jesus was now back to His normal self.

Jesus only

The whole point of the speaker's message could be summed up in those two words, "Jesus only." He was saying, "We are to look to Jesus and to Jesus only. He is the Author and Finisher of our faith, the Alpha and the Omega, the Beginning and the End. His is the only name under heaven by which we can be saved. He is the Head of His Body, the Church. He is the Bridegroom. He is everything and His name is supreme." It was all about Jesus and Jesus only!

Now when he preached that, everything in me said, "Amen!" because Jesus had saved me and I had had such a powerful experience of salvation. Jesus had become everything to me. Every time I would pray it was always addressed to "Jesus my Lord." Everything was Jesus. Worship was all about Jesus. The songs we sung were all about Jesus.

Sometimes they would put a verse in about the Holy Spirit or about the Father but everything was focused on the person of Jesus and I thought that was the whole focus of Christianity.

"HAVE YOU RECEIVED THE *FATHER'S* LOVE?"

Some years later we went to Bible School, and a man called Jack Winter came to New Zealand and spoke at a conference in the school. Jack began to speak about the Father and during that time he began to receive a greater revelation of the Father. We had never met anybody with the anointing of God upon them like Jack had. We had been exposed to a lot of wonderful ministry but, as far as I was concerned, when Jack Winter spoke it was like listening to Jesus. It was way beyond anything else that I had heard before.

Jack used to say a wonderful thing: "Many people preach the gospel *but we give them an opportunity to live it.*" That was a huge statement. To join Jack's ministry you would sell up everything you owned and give it to the poor or lay it at the apostles' feet and follow together with the body of Christians that was called Daystar Ministries at that time. It was the most pure faith ministry that I have ever seen. There were times when the two hundred people on the base had no food whatsoever for the next meal so we just prayed. It is one thing to pray and intercede for something, but when you need food on the table within two hours, it puts a whole different level to the reality of what is going on in your prayers.

The revelation about the Father that had begun to occur to Jack at the conference in New Zealand was now in full bloom and he had come to realize that if people had an experience of the Father's love they would receive emotional healing. It was an exciting time. There was something like four hundred families who applied to join his ministry that year. There were twelve different bases throughout the United States and they had six hundred full-time staff, yet Jack's desk was a little table beside his bed. He was not into anything grandiose, whatsoever.

When we arrived there, everybody was really excited about this revelation of the Father's love and started to ask me, "Have you received the Father's love?" I was so offended by that! I was twenty-eight years old and felt that we would spend the rest of our lives in Jack's ministry. I was right out of the New Zealand bush, which most people would describe as jungle. Three and a half thousand feet up a mountainside the bush turns to tussock land, which is like oceans of golden grasses. Those hills are beautiful places to spend your life, and I came from this very outdoor kind of life, fit and strong as a young man. I was accustomed to living in the hills, sleeping out in the open, chopping wood for the fire to cook my meals, and I was hardened to that kind of life. And now people were asking me, "Have you received the Father's love?"

My inner response to this question was somewhat irate, "Look, I'm filled with the Holy Spirit. I've planted a church already. I've been to Bible School. I can prophesy, cast out demons, heal the sick and preach the gospel on the streets. I'm a demon destroyer. I'm a man of God! God has called me to be a prophet, to be a sharp threshing instrument that divides between soul and spirit! My words will bring people to their knees! My preaching will divide the sinner from the righteous and speak into the lives of many people! I'm called to be a prophet. I'm not into this "love stuff." What do you mean, *'Am I filled with the Father's love?'*"

FIRST LIGHT

After we had been there a few months a thought occurred to me out of the blue. I remembered when I was four years old, my mother (who must have had some touch of the Lord in her life back then), over a brief period of time, used to take my brother and sister and me into her bedroom at night, and we would kneel down in front of a little chest where she had a cross and a candle. She would light the candle and then she taught us the Lord's Prayer. In later years they couldn't remember that but I remembered it very well because from that time onwards I prayed the Lord's Prayer every night when I went to bed. I would close my eyes, and in my mind I would pray the Lord's Prayer. At the end I would always pray, "God, bless Mum and Dad, my brother Bob, and my sister Sylvia, and Lord, when I grow up let me be healthy, have a happy family and a good job." I prayed that every night. Some nights I missed so the next night I prayed it twice! I never missed a night.

During those first few months at Daystar, the Lord reminded me that when Jesus taught His disciples to pray, He taught them to say, "Our Father." I realized I had been praying that from when I was four until I was about fourteen or fifteen! Jesus taught the disciples to speak to His *Father*. I could see now that Jesus, even at the very beginning, was directing the disciples into a relationship directly with the Father, and not just with *Him*. This was the first crack, so to speak, in that message of "Jesus only" that I had heard. I was beginning to realize that Christianity was not only about Jesus.

You see, when people would say to me, "Have you received the Father's love?" the question for me was, "Why are you talking about the Father? It's all about Jesus! His is the only name under heaven by which we can be saved. He is Lord of all. He is the King of kings. It's all about Him. He's the one who saved us, the one who died on the cross." I didn't realize that the Father also died on the cross in a very real sense; I just kept repeating, "It's all about Jesus!"

I was feeling that if I had a relationship with the Father then I was being disloyal to Jesus. I thought to myself, "After all that Jesus has done for me, how can I turn my back on Jesus and relate to the

Father?" That was the struggle for me. Of course that has nothing to do with it, but that is how I felt. This memory of praying "Our Father" was the first breach in my defenses. Jesus actually told the disciples to talk to their Father. He said,

"But you, when you pray go into your room and when you have shut your door, pray to your Father." (Matthew 6:6).

Suddenly I was thinking, "Oh! There *is* something about the Father in this." It *is* legitimate to have direct interaction with the Father. I was beginning to make some ground.

WORSHIPPING THE FATHER

A few months later another crack appeared. I remembered the time some years previously, when I was in Bible School and we had a lecturer from America who brought his family to be with him there. This guy spent eleven years at the school and he gave lectures on the Gospel of John. There were times after his teaching when, instead of walking out of the classroom, we would almost float out of the classroom! The reverence and worship with which he taught was such an incredible blessing. He took us through the book of John verse by verse for a whole year. At the end of the year he apologized that we had only managed to get to Chapter 16! It had been an incredible year of looking deeply into the book of John.

However, when we got to Chapter 4, he said, "We're going to do this chapter differently. Instead of me teaching, I am going to give each of you one or two verses for you to study and then come back and present to the class what you have learned." When he said that I immediately hoped that I would be given one particular verse. I thought that if I got that verse I wouldn't have to do any homework because I had already got revelation on that verse. I was very busy, so if I got that particular verse I could avoid doing homework and would be able to grab some spare time for myself.

So he allotted verses to each member of the class and he gave me exactly the verse that I was hoping for. The verse was John 4:23, but when I had studied this verse this is what I thought it said, "A time is coming and is now coming when the true worshippers will worship God in spirit and in truth, for these are the kind of worshippers that God seeks." This is not exactly what it says, but this is what I *thought* it said. I was so pleased that I had been given the verse I wanted. I didn't need to study it. Finally it came to my turn to share my revelation in front of the class. I was confident that I had done a good job in communicating the understanding of the verse, and this was confirmed when some of the students came up to me afterwards and complimented me.

My revelation was about "worship in spirit and truth" because I knew what worship is. Worship is when your spirit tries to come out of your mouth and is a total expression of love and adoration. There isn't much thinking in it; it is just a connection of spirit. I have discovered that you cannot learn to worship. Worship is a natural response to His presence. *That* is worship in spirit and in truth! And that was what I had shared as my revelation into this word.

Then, eight years later, I discovered what the verse *really* meant. In the verse Jesus actually said,

"A time is coming and has now come when the true worshippers will worship <u>the Father</u> in spirit and in truth for these are the kind of worshippers <u>the Father</u> seeks."

Until this time my whole focus of worship was on the person of Jesus and Jesus only. All the songs we used to sing in those days, and even now are 'Jesus only' focused. We wear those WWJD (What Would Jesus Do?) wristbands. We sing, "It's all about You, Jesus." Somehow I don't think that Jesus would agree with those statements. I believe that Jesus would say, "It's *actually* all about My Father."

Of course, it is not wrong to worship Jesus. Some of the greatest verses about worship in Scripture are about the person of Jesus, particularly in Revelation, where all the elders throw their crowns before Him, lifting up the Lamb of God in worship. But the point I wish to make here is that Jesus *Himself* said, "The true worshippers will worship *the Father* in spirit and in truth." At the time when I read that I could not imagine saying, "I worship You, Father" or, "I love You, Father." I was shocked that these words were so far from my perspective but I could see that Jesus Himself said them. I was beginning to realise that there is actually a place for the Father in our lives! My "Jesus and Jesus only" stance was beginning to shift.

As this whole revelation is beginning to come into the church in these days, and as we are beginning to see the Father again, there are people who are struggling with this same issue and they often make the criticism that, "You guys seem to just go to the Father and bypass Jesus." Let me say this very clearly. In no way do we bypass Jesus. The only *Way* to the Father is through Jesus and it is only in Him that we have a relationship with the Father.

We are in Christ

Some say that heresy is often sung before it is preached. I really wish that people who write Christian songs would consult with someone who actually has some biblical understanding. Often our songs are not what the Bible teaches at all, yet we often sing the songs more than we read the Scriptures. For example, there is an old hymn that talks about, "...walking with Jesus the light of the world." Many songs talk about "walking with Jesus" but that is not really a biblical statement.

We do not walk *with* Jesus. We are *in* Christ and He is *in* us. Our life has been swallowed up in His life. We are baptized into Him and now it is, "*...no longer I who live but Christ who lives in me, and the life that I now live I live by faith of the Son of God who loved me and gave Himself for me.*" (Galatians 2:20) He has become my life. He lives *within* me and I am *in* Him. I have been baptized *into* Him. It is not so much that I walk with Him side by side, but He is *in* me and I am in Him. The reality is that we walk with the *Father* in Christ. In reality it is not actually *my* relationship with the Father. I have entered into *Jesus'* relationship with *His* Father.

JESUS IS THE WAY TO THE FATHER

Throughout this whole process I began to see that it is actually biblical to have a personal relationship with the Father because of who Jesus is and who I am *in* Him.

And then I came across John chapter 14 and this is worth pondering because there is something here that is often misunderstood. I love the verses telling of the last few days before Jesus was crucified. Jack Winter's observation was that the final utterances of a person prior to their death are especially worthy of attention.

Jesus began by saying,

"Let not your heart be troubled. You believe in God, believe also in Me. In My Father's house are many mansions. If it were not so, I would have told you. I go to prepare a place for you. And if I go and prepare a place for you, I will come again and receive you to Myself, that where I am, there you may be also," (v1-3).

Jesus was announcing that He was leaving yet the disciples were still hoping for a literal kingdom. It was quite a shock for them because Jesus said, "I'm going. I'm leaving you here." I can imagine them looking at one another and saying, "Did *you* know about *this*? I came and followed Him because I thought He was going to oust the Romans. We have given our lives and left our fishing nets. We were going to raise up a kingdom like the Maccabees did and we would become soldiers of a new army to break the bondage and set Israel free. What is He talking about *now*?"

But Jesus basically said, "No, I go to prepare a place for you but you cannot come with Me right now." Then He continued,

"Where I go, you know, and the way you know." (John 14:4)

I remember being at school with thirty students in the class with me. Sometimes the teacher would make a statement that none of us understood, but nobody said anything because nobody wanted to ask a question that made him or her look stupid. I imagine that the disciples had a similar reaction when Jesus said, "You know where I am going and you know the way." I can imagine that these guys were looking at each other thinking, "Do you know? Did He tell you? He didn't tell me. Was I away that day? What is He talking about? "

I am sure that each was ashamed to admit that they didn't

actually know. Thomas then made this beautifully pure and innocent statement, "Lord, we do not know where You are going. How can we know the way?" I'm so glad Thomas said that because if he didn't we wouldn't have the next verse, which is one of the major verses of the New Testament,

"Jesus said to him 'I am the way, the truth and the life. No-one comes to the Father except through Me."(John 14:6).

He was telling them the way and the destination! When He said, "I am going to prepare a place for you so that where I am you may be also," what He was really saying was that He was going to prepare a place for them in the Father's heart. Note that He did *not* say, "...You *will be* where I will be," but rather He said, "You will be where *I am.*" Jesus always lived eternally in the bosom of the Father and while He was on earth He was *still* living there. John 1:18 says,

"No one has seen God at any time. The only begotten Son who is in the bosom of the Father, He has declared Him."

There is a time coming when the world will only listen to those who are dwelling in the bosom of the Father, in His love. Because it is only from that place that we can really declare God, really reveal Him to the world. Sonship is going to overcome every other perspective of Christianity. It *has* to, because only then will the Church finally become the total representation of the Son of God.

FATHER IS THE DESTINATION

Jesus said, "*I am the way, the truth and the life, no one comes to the Father but by Me,*" Jesus is the Way to the destination. The *destination* is the Father. Then He added this statement,

"If you had really known Me, you would have known My Father also and from now on you know Him and have seen Him."

Many people have taken these words and believed that if you have seen Jesus, if you have an experiential and real relationship with Him, then you automatically have a relationship with the Father. They believe that there is no separate experience of the Father other than your contact with Jesus. I could almost believe the same if it wasn't for verse 8, and Philip's question here,

"Philip said to Him, 'Lord, show us the Father and that will be sufficient for us.'"

What Philip was basically saying is, "Jesus, I've been watching You for three years. I can see You but I can't see the Father!" We see that You have relationship with Him but we can only see You. Show us the *Father!*"

Jesus replied,

"Have I been with you so long and yet you have not known Me, Philip? He who has seen Me has seen the Father, so how can you say 'Show us the Father'? Do you not believe that I am in the Father and the Father is in Me? The words that I speak to you, I do not speak on My own authority but My Father who dwells in Me does the works. Believe Me that I am in the Father and the Father is in Me, or else believe Me for the sake of the works themselves."

He was telling Philip that the miracles were actually signs of the Father's presence. In verse 7, He said, "If you had really known Me, you would have known the Father also," (NIV). In other words, "You can know Me or you can *really* know Me, and if you *really* knew Me you would see the Father as well."

The truth, dear reader, is that you can have a relationship with Jesus - and yet not "see" the Father at all.

FATHER HAS TO BE REVEALED BY JESUS

Let me put it another way. Jesus made another statement in Matthew 11:27. He said,

"All things have been delivered to Me by My Father and no one knows the Son except the Father. Nor does anyone know the Father except the Son, and the one to whom the Son wills to reveal Him."

This statement really touched me as a young person, because I had always thought that loneliness is when you don't know anybody. I discovered however that the true definition of loneliness is when nobody knows *you*. When you perceive that nobody really knows what it is like to be you then you are in a very lonely place. Loneliness is broken when you can let somebody else know what it is like to live your life.

When Jesus said in this verse, "Nobody knows the Son except the Father," He was really saying that God was the only one who really knew Him. Jesus carried this loneliness all of His life on this earth. Not even His mother understood Him. She "pondered these things in her heart" but she didn't really understand Him. He said, "Only the Father *really* knows Me." Then He turned the statement around, "Nor does anyone really know the Father except the Son."

This was one of the reasons why the Jewish leaders got angry with Him and crucified Him. Because this Jesus from Nazareth claimed to know Yahweh better than *them*, the religious elite! These leaders had spent their entire life in the temple from boyhood onwards and had learned everything that is possible to know about God! They had lived in this environment continually, memorizing vast portions of Scripture, defining their behavior so that they never did anything wrong, for the purpose that they might know God and be approved by Him.

Now this carpenter's son, who was in all likelihood labelled as an illegitimate child, came to them and said, "In all of your learning you don't actually know Yahweh. *Only I do.*" Obviously they thought that He was crazy, arrogant, or the ultimate heretic. He condemned the whole Jewish religious system by saying that He was the only one who got it right, the only one who really knew God.

And He was right. They may have known *about* God but He *knew* God. You see, because He was not born a son of Adam, sin did not separate Him from God. Isaiah 59:2 tells us that sin separates us from God but Jesus was *born* sinless! He wasn't a son of Adam. He was a direct conception of God Himself in the womb of Mary.

Contact with God was automatically available throughout His life. Whenever He prayed, His Father was revealed to Him - *spirit to spirit*. He still had to walk it out by faith just as we do but He had an intimate connection with the Father. He was naturally conceived of the Spirit so He was filled with the Holy Spirit from the very point of conception.

So when He said, "Nobody knows the Father except Me," He was actually saying, "The whole Jewish race and those who have learned all about Him don't actually know Him but I do!" He proved the truth of this by the works that He did and the words that He said. The works that He did were to be a sign of the Father's presence, not just an exercise of His power and authority. His miracles pointed to the reality of the love that the Father has for us.

As the religious leaders were reeling from His audacious claim to be the only one who actually knew God, He expanded His statement, "No one knows the Father except the Son *and the one to whom the Son chooses to reveal Him.*" What He meant was, "I know the Father by personal connection, and no one knows Him like I do, *but* I can reveal Him to you. I can reveal the Father to those to whom I choose to reveal Him." The Father needs to be revealed to us by Jesus!

IT IS A REVELATION

There is a *revelation* of the Father. You cannot simply come to know the Father because you have a desire to. You cannot come to know the Father because you appropriate something in Scripture or believe what the Scripture says. The Father has to be revealed to you by revelation, just as Jesus was revealed to you by revelation when you were born again.

You were not born again by your own power. There is nothing that you did that caused you to be saved. You responded to God's initiative.

Repentance and faith do not in themselves cause you to be born again. However, when God sees that you are doing that fully from your heart, He causes a spiritual transaction to occur in your spirit, rebirthing you on the inside. It's not just because you believe what the Bible says and you try to do what the Bible says. You become a new creation by supernatural means. Something brand new has been born in you and you are not the same anymore. It is God's work in your heart. Salvation is actually a revelation of Jesus and that revelation is given by God Himself. He shows Jesus to us.

Similarly, the baptism of the Spirit is when the Holy Spirit is revealed to your spirit. The reality of the Holy Spirit, the substance of His being, is manifested to the deepest part of who you are in your spirit, and you suddenly know that the Holy Spirit is real. We call it the "baptism of the Spirit," or the "filling of the Spirit," but it really is your spirit getting a revelation of the presence of the Holy Spirit within you. When that happens you receive revelation and the knowledge of some truths comes to you automatically.

When you meet Jesus in salvation there are some truths that get imparted to you supernaturally and you have absolutely no doubts as to the veracity of them. You will *know* that Jesus was born of the Virgin Mary. How do you know that? By *revelation* of the Lord, because that is who Jesus is. You will know that He is not merely *a* son of God. He is *the* Son of God and you know without question that there is no other son apart from Jesus. Your innermost spirit has met Him and you know that undeniable reality. Many martyrs died horrendous deaths because they could not deny the revelation and reality of Jesus.

The baptism of the Holy Spirit also brings *revelation* knowledge that He gives miraculous power. Samson pulled down the pillars of the temple. Elijah outran chariots and horses to get back to the city. When the Spirit of God comes upon a person, power also comes upon them because the Spirit of God administers the power of

God. The Godhead was personally involved in the creation of the universe. The Father initiated, He spoke the Word, which is Jesus, and the power of the Holy Spirit created, the Trinity all working together.

If you are not filled with the Holy Spirit you will seek explanations for miracles that diminish their reality, but when you are filled with the Spirit it is different. You truly know because you have touched the reality of the One who has the power of God.

THE REVELATION OF THE FATHER

Knowing the Father is not just a matter of adhering to a theology in the book, but the Father Himself becomes real to your spirit and His love begins to be revealed within you. When Jesus said, "No one knows the Father except Me and those to whom I choose to reveal Him," He is talking about a *revealing* of God our Father to our hearts.

We are entering into a realm of the heart as we come into this because *revelation* comes to your heart. I love this because it is not just for the intellectual and those with strong enough willpower to do the things that they are supposed to do. In fact, those things mostly get in the way.

I believe God is now pouring out a revelation of Himself as Father in a way that is unprecedented since the time of the apostles. The whole point of Christianity is to know the Father and to know Him by revelation. Jesus is the Way to the Father. The revealing of the Father is the destination.

CHAPTER 2

Why the Heart Matters

~

Let me encourage you to allow the Spirit of God to feed your spirit as you read this book. My desire is that through this book God would do a work in your heart. This is my focus in writing. God generally does not come and re-indoctrinate your mind. What He does, however, is that He comes and He *changes our hearts*, because when your heart is changed you are a different person. Without needing to do anything else you will act differently and be a different person. When the heart is changed you will *automatically* act differently.

I'm sure you have noticed that the Bible is not written as a textbook. It doesn't have a list of subjects with capital letters listing the topics in order. It is purposely written by God in such a way that the truths have to be discovered by those who have eyes to see and hears. I once heard somebody saying that God loves to be found! Like a father playing "hide and seek" with his children, He has planned that only those who will come and spend time with

Him, with a hunger to find Him, will discover Him.

As we read the Bible, seeking Him with all our hearts there, He will show us great and mighty things that we didn't know about. It is when we call out to Him that He answers! His truths are hidden to the casual observer. That is why He hasn't given His word to us as a textbook that the casual observer can discover. Its truths are hidden in words that appear just like all the others.

I have discovered a maxi-truth hidden in Proverbs 4:23. This says, *"Keep your heart with all diligence, for out of it spring the issues of life."* Another translation puts it; *"Guard your heart with all diligence, for it is the wellspring of life."* This verse has become a major focus for our ministry and I believe that it is one of the big statements of Scripture. The Bible is full of these maxi-truth statements such as "God is love," or "God is a Spirit." These are major issues - they are maxi-truths! I really believe that this verse in Proverbs 4 is one of the maxi-truths of Christianity, which sadly has been overlooked by most Christians today.

You see, your heart is the most important part of you, and everything that you experience life to be is experienced through your heart. The way that you interpret life, the way that you interpret events and how they affect you is all determined by the condition of your heart. The truth is, your mind is yours – your emotions are yours – your will is yours – but your heart is *you!*

I illustrate it like this. One person can say something to two people at the same time yet one listener can interpret it to mean one thing while the second listener can interpret it to mean something else. The person speaking can be using the same words, spoken at the same time to these two people, yet they can mean two very different things to the two listeners. Why? It is because their hearts have been conditioned differently, and those words mean different things to different people. Two people may experience the same look from a person and interpret it entirely differently.

In fact, you could say that we all live in different worlds because each of our hearts has been conditioned to experience life differently. For example, when a boy who has been brought up with a violent father hears the word "father" his heart will automatically be closed off to that word. He will not listen to what you are saying. But when a boy who has a wonderful father hears the word "father" it will immediately evoke feelings of comfort and security. Two completely different worlds!

Each one of us lives in a different world simply because our hearts have been changed and affected by the things that we have lived through. Our family environment, the part of the world we grew up in, cultural attitudes, our schooling, our intellectual status, our athletic ability, and our different relationships. All these things have affected the way that we now experience life. You may not even be able to articulate what you think, but you see life through the conditioning of your heart.

How our hearts are changed

When we became Christians we wanted to change and become more like Jesus. God's way of doing this, however, is not through the education of your mind, or to motivate you to make better decisions through human determination. Yet this is often the way that Christian maturity has been presented to us. "If you want to change, then you have got to do it this way. You have to mature. You have to grow."

The predominant understanding of discipleship, as we are often told today, goes something like this. *"You have to do this, and you have to do that"* or, *"You must stop doing this, and you must stop doing that"* or again, *"You have to develop these habit patterns and develop this behaviour in order to change."*

The truth is, even if you can stop yourself from doing a certain action, this doesn't change your true self because your heart makes you who you really are! The way that your heart has been affected by your life experiences determines who you are at this time.

This is why Proverbs 4:23 says,

"Keep your heart with all diligence, for from it spring the issues of life."

Everything that you are is because of the condition of your heart. You may be able to change your behaviour by determination and willpower, but I can tell you what will happen. You may make the right choices and do everything the way you are supposed to do. You may even learn to smile the right kind of smile and behave like a good Christian. But one day something will happen in your world and you will suddenly go back to who you *really* are, using language that you know you shouldn't use. Or you will revert to a way of thinking and a way of treating people that you know is wrong.

In a moment of extreme stress it will come out of your mouth. You may even say, "I'm so sorry, that was not me." Let me tell you the truth... *that is really you.* Because, when the pressure is on, what is really in your heart will come out in what you say and the manner in which you say it. When everything is nice and comfortable you can speak from your mind and know the right things to say, but when the pressure is on, you will speak and act out of the true condition of your heart. Changing your actions will not change who you are in your true self. Real and lasting change is a changed heart.

Thankfully, God is in the business of changing our hearts. I love this statement; it is such a wonderful truth. *When God changes your heart, that part of your heart will automatically fulfill everything that God asks of you. You will automatically be what a Christian should be without thinking about it, because it will come out of your heart.*

In Fatherheart Ministries in Norway, we have a wonderful couple called Olav and Unni. They were saved in the 1970's and the impact in their town in Norway was remarkable. A third of the young people in the town became Christians. We first met them about ten years ago when we ministered at their church and the love of the Father affected them deeply. All of Olav's striving to perform, to be "the good Christian man," to be "the good pastor," stopped when he experienced the Father's love and entered into rest. The love of the Father has transformed their lives.

Olav and Unni do a significant amount of ministry in Kenya. When they were walking home from a meeting one night in Nairobi, nine young men accosted them, beat them severely and stole everything they had. They left them lying in the middle of a dirt road in the slums of Nairobi. When they regained consciousness, Unni was overjoyed to find that she still had her wedding ring but everything else was gone. They could only crawl to each other, but as they began to pray for their attackers they were both filled with such love for these men who had beaten them! This amazed them. Love just flowed out from them. They couldn't think anything else but, "These lovely young men, God help them and love them. They are such wonderful young men. God bless them." All of this love came out of their hearts. This experience convinced them of the absolute reality of the Father's love, because the love flowed from their hearts without any effort at all. They didn't have to forgive their attackers because they had discovered that they possessed something much greater. They possessed a deep love for their enemies.

This is what a true Christian heart should be! It is not that, "I must forgive them" or, "I know the right thing is to forgive them." For Olav and Unni it was an overwhelming expression of what was already in their hearts. They didn't have to ask themselves what the right thing was to do in that situation. The same kind of heart that Jesus would have shown was automatically in them!

When God changes your heart, you will automatically be different.

Christianity is not about learning how to act and then by human determination trying to do it. I believe, of course, that we should resist sinning with all our determination, but stopping sinning is not Christlikeness. We must realize that it is only God who can change our hearts to become a Christlike person. When He changes you, you will automatically be different without even thinking about it.

We need to understand that Christianity is self-energised. When you live a Christian life it will turn you into everything a Christian can and should be. It will not be you who does it. Not your efforts, self-control or discipline. If you develop a life that looks like a Christian one, by your own efforts, then *you* will take the glory for it. It is only when God has changed you *Himself* that you will give all the glory to Him for it. God works in our hearts to change what we are and, there and then, all of our behaviours and ways of thinking *automatically* change to be like the One who changed us.

SCAR TISSUE

If you have been deeply wounded in your life, it is a wound in your heart and it will stay there until God heals it. As long as the wound is there, that part of you will be bent and twisted in some way and will not operate how it is supposed to.

I fell off my bicycle when I was nine years of age and was left with a scar across my knee, where the rusty handle cut into my skin. I cried and cried. When I got home I could see a great cut across my knee. As my mother was cleaning it, my father looked at it and said, "You will have that scar for the rest of your life." The scar is still there today but it is very small. Do you know why? My knee grew! Yet the scar stayed the same size because scar tissue does not grow. When your heart is scarred, that part of you does not grow up but remains a child. This is why so many of us sometimes have childish reactions that we are ashamed of. We are determined to react differently the next time but invariably we react in the same way! God is in the business of healing the scars in your heart. When He heals a scar in your heart, that part of you grows back into maturity. It does not take a long time for it to grow again either. Thankfully, God heals us very quickly!

When your heart has been neglected or has not received the affection that it needs, or when it has been broken and hurt, then that part of your heart will remain scarred until God heals it. God's work is to heal our hearts and He does it by pouring in His comforting love.

YOUR HEART IS YOU

When you get wounded in your heart, the deepest part of you is wounded. Why? Because your heart is not yours. Your heart is *you*. Your ability to make choices is an ability that you have, because your will is yours. You can direct your will however you like. You are not your mind, because you can change your mind. You can decide to think differently. Therefore what you think is not you, because you have control over what you think. You can educate your mind in different ways. You can know that something is wrong but decide to believe something else. You can direct your own mind. Your mind is not you. It is yours.

It is the same with your emotions. Your emotions are yours, but they are not *you*. Many people get trapped into thinking that their emotions are actually who they are. When they feel sad, then the whole world is sad. If they feel happy, then life is wonderful. If they feel depressed, then they see the world as a depressed place. Your feelings and emotions may be yours but they are not who you really are. Just because you feel a certain way, it does not make it true.

Your mind is yours, your will is yours, your feelings are yours. *Your heart is you.*

HEALING LOVE

When God changes your heart, you begin to love what God loves. You begin to feel as God feels. You begin to think like God thinks. You begin to do what God does - automatically! So this book is not about education, but rather that He would come into your heart to heal it and pour His love in, and change your heart to be like His.

The wonderful news is that when love comes in, everything that the *lack of* love has done to you is reversed. Sometimes I use the word 'un-love', which may not be a real word but it describes the reality well. There are so many things in this world that we have experienced that are not love. You may have had many traumatic experiences of un-love, which have created holes in the foundation of your life. Each experience of un-love is like an explosion in the deepest part of your being. When God pours His love onto that foundation, it automatically fills the holes first. His love runs into the holes and the traumas of your life and begins to make you whole.

Yet most of us still do not understand this. The focus of most of the counselling ministry that we did was to diagnose the brokenness in a person's life by attempting to identify and isolate incidents through which they were wounded. We would then pray into that issue, for God to heal it and God answered our prayers and came to pour in His healing love. So it was successful. What I have discovered now, however, is that if you can open your heart and just allow the love of the Father to come in, it will fill *all* the holes! You don't have to go and identify them. It just runs into them automatically! So if we can find the key to help each one of us open our hearts to allow the Father's love to come in, and to keep that love flowing, we are going to get healed whether we like it or not!

You see, the love of the Father pours into your heart and this is the place where you meet Him. I once thought there was nothing more to the ministry than that. We used to believe that the Father Heart of God message is something that heals people emotionally but I have discovered that the healing of the heart is just the introduction to knowing the Father. When His love first comes in it will heal our hearts. If we keep our hearts open we can become sons and daughters in relationship with the Father, growing in the knowledge and experience of His love.

The key is really about opening our hearts. I don't know how to open my heart. I have no idea how it actually happens. I wish I did. But what I *can* do is to simply lay myself down before God and say, "God, whatever You want to do is okay with me. However much it might hurt, do it anyway. Father, I trust that You are a good God and You will not harm me. I can surrender myself to You. I can trust You because You are good."

Many of us have reasons why we cannot trust some people in our lives. There is never a reason not to trust God. Some people say, "God allowed this to happen in my life." God never did anything wrong to you, or anyone else – ever! He can only be good. He cannot sin. So there is never a reason for us to hold an offence against God or to forgive Him for something that we may feel that He did. We may believe that He did something wrong, but He did not. Even though we may not always understand what happens in our lives, the truth is that God is always and only good.

As you read this book, I invite you to surrender your heart to Him, as much as you know how. You can say, "Father, here I am, for whatever You would like to do." Maybe you are reading this with your own expectations but I would rather that God's expectations are fulfilled instead of my own. You can say, "Father, I am here for what *You* want for me, not for my own expectations to be met."

He is only good. We can trust Him.

CHAPTER 3

Forgiving from the Heart

~

When Jesus died on the cross, He said, "It is finished!" Everything that God can do for us has already been done. Everything that God has in His heart for us is now provided. The situation is that we are now coming into the realization of what He has done. What Jesus accomplished on the cross is becoming real in our experience. The process of Christian growth is all about you and me entering into the reality of what He has already done. God doesn't need to do any more. Christ has done it all. But why can we not enter fully into that? Over the next two chapters I want to explore the answer to this.

HE IS ALREADY LOVING US

In this whole revelation of the Father's love, the issue is not that we are trying to get Him to pour His love into our hearts. His love is continually raining down upon us every moment. The question is, *"Why am I not experiencing that more? Why is it not real to me?"*

The main issue facing us is that there are blockages within us that hinder that reality from becoming our life. As we get rid of those blockages His love for us becomes more and more real in our experience. The theme song of the Welsh revival was a beautiful hymn, "Here is love vast as the ocean, loving kindness as a flood." The love of God is like an ocean. I know what oceans are like. It takes almost twelve hours to fly from New Zealand to Los Angeles and there is basically nothing between but ocean. We are just beginning to dip our toes into the amazing ocean of the Father's love.

When we enter into the continuous experiencing of Him loving us, this changes our personality. It changes our life and transforms us into the image of Jesus. *The love itself transforms us.* The key to spiritual growth is to get rid of the things that hinder us from experiencing the reality of His love. That is the most simple yet the most profound truth.

CHRISTIANITY IS SELF-ENERGIZED

Christianity is *self-energized* from the inside out. If you are living real Christianity it will create a Christian in you, transforming you to be everything that Jesus is. You do not have to *do anything* to make that happen. If you are not being transformed into the likeness of Jesus, the reality is that you are not actually experiencing Christianity. The essence of Christianity is simply this: Jesus died on the cross to reconcile us to God, so that we can enter into relationship with His Father and live in the experience of the Father loving us continuously. Christianity is infinitely more than the conceptual knowledge that God loves you. It is the *actual* experience of being *loved* by Him every minute of every day. The difference between these two realities is massive. Even the devil knows that God loves you. That is not faith; it's just correct doctrine. Faith is *knowing* Him *loving* you. If you are not experiencing that it is because of blockages in your heart. When the blockages are removed there is an open heaven.

Christianity can be likened to a person who has inherited a lot of money from a relative who has died, but who is unaware of it. Some years ago the New Zealand media carried a story about a man who had inherited a huge amount of money from a distant relative in South America whom he had never even heard of. It took the executors of the estate some years to determine that he was the only living relative and to subsequently track him down. He had inherited the staggering sum of thirteen billion dollars.

Imagine the scenario. One day he gets a telephone call from a lawyer, summoning him to a meeting. He goes to the meeting and learns that this vast sum of money is now entirely his. What a shock! What do you think he would do the next day? This would change his life dramatically and permanently. You could spend hours imagining what he would do and how his life would be changed.

The truth, dear reader, is that this is exactly what Christianity is like. Through the death and resurrection of Jesus we have come into a huge inheritance. So many of us have got little idea of what that really is, but we are learning. We are finding out what it really means to be saved. It is so much more than just getting a ticket to heaven, living a nice life, being kind to the neighbours, being a good employer or employee, going to church on a regular basis or even having a ministry in the church. Many believe that is the sum total of what Christianity is! Let me tell you, Christianity is just a little bit bigger!

Christianity is about you and I becoming like Jesus! That is the purpose. To live a life in eternity conformed to the life that Jesus lives in eternity. It is far beyond what we can imagine! Christianity is a huge thing and we have inherited the whole lot. The person who has been a Christian for five minutes has inherited no less than the person who has been a Christian for eighty-five years. The person who has been a Christian longer may understand more of what his inheritance is, but we all actually possess the same thing.

Einstein once said, "You don't really know what you can't explain to your grandmother." I really like that, because when you really know something in life it becomes simple. What I am talking about is not complicated. The Father loves us and it changes who we are. As we know that love, experience that love, and walk in that love, it transforms us into the image of the Lord. So I want to tell you some of the things that have been blockages in my own life and point out the path that the Lord has taken me down to get there.

AN UNCOMFORTABLE MIRACLE

We first met Jack Winter in New Zealand in 1976 when he invited us to come and be a part of his ministry in the States, known as Daystar Ministries. We went there in September 1978, flying into a stiflingly hot Los Angeles, and then to Indianapolis. We had come on a one-way ticket, which I thought was a wonderful miracle of God because to enter the United States as a short or long-term visitor you must be able to show a return ticket. Dorothy Winter picked us up at the airport, and we went to their ministry centre in Martinsville, Indiana. It was there that we began to hear about the Father's love.

I had a big problem, however. I really didn't feel like I was called to a ministry of love. I was a man of God, not a wimp of God. This "love stuff" definitely wasn't for me. For me, ministry was about being "a sharp threshing instrument" with words that cut through the powers of evil, and brought the demons to their knees. When I got to Jack's ministry centre, with Denise and the three children, I was dismayed to discover that it was all about this "love stuff." I feared that we had made a terrible mistake but we couldn't go home because we didn't have a return ticket! The Lord had His purposes in the midst of my discomfort.

So we were stuck there, and after a short while I began to think about what I could do to make the time there more worthwhile. Then, as I was speaking to one of their intercessors one day, I looked into her eyes and I could see that she really knew how to pray. I thought, "I've got no idea how to pray but she obviously does." So I decided there and then that I would try to learn.

LEARNING TO PRAY LIKE A REAL MAN

I was very motivated by a story in the book of Acts where Peter was up on a roof and it says that while he was praying, he became hungry. I thought, "How long does it take to for a man to get hungry?" It must take at least a few hours. I related to Peter in the sense that he was a physical and hardworking man. A man with calloused hands and a weather-beaten face. An outdoors guy like myself. The type of man who, when things went wrong, would self-medicate through work. He went fishing after Jesus died. He didn't crawl under the bed to mourn or shut himself away to read poetry. I love poetry and have written some myself but it was the workman in Peter that I identified more with. My hands were calloused too. I had spent a lot of my life in the mountains as a professional hunter and then worked as a builder after Denise and I got married.

So I could identify with this rough and tough man, Peter. Even an outdoor, active, and hardworking person like him learned how to have stamina in his prayer life. Sometimes we assume that it is easier for an introvert or a scholarly type to pray with longevity yet here was Peter praying until he got hungry. This challenged me greatly.

Another biblical character that challenged me was Elijah who was evidently a hard type of man also. He is described as having a "forehead like flint." It takes a certain kind of person to be able to do the things that he did. If Elijah walked into the room we would probably be scared of his eyes. What struck me was that (in 2 Kings 1:9) he was sitting on a hill. To me, this indicated that he had a prayer life. He knew how to just sit with God.

I was challenged that I didn't know how to pray for any length of time. So I wanted to learn to pray. My goal was to become more like these inspirational characters that I had read about. In the basement of the place where we were living there was a beautiful little chapel that was decorated entirely in green, so I thought that I would spend some time there each Saturday morning when no one else was around. I planned to close the door, stay there and pray for as long as I could.

As the following Saturday drew near I was thinking up lists of things to pray for. Anything that could generally be described as prayer would be called upon just to make it last longer. I thought that if my mind wandered I would not condemn myself but just refocus my thoughts. I was at peace that I wasn't going to ask forgiveness for my human frailty but I would just work my way down the list of requests. The next Saturday morning I closed myself in the chapel and prayed for everything that I could think of.

I prayed in tongues, I prayed in English, I prayed singing, I prayed lying on my face, I prayed lying on my back, I prayed running around the room. I prayed as long as I could, and as slowly as possible to make it last longer. I had my Bible with me but I was there to pray not read the Bible. After what seemed like an eternity, the walls were closing in on me. I was bored and becoming claustrophobic. I rushed to the door and went into the corridor. I looked at my watch and it was 6:20 am. I had started at 6:00 am.

Now, I'm not a person to give up easily. That was the reality of learning to pray. Throughout the rest of the week I was thinking of more things to pray for. I would go down again the next Saturday because I had committed myself to go each Saturday. The next Saturday I went through the same process, praying for everything I could think of, as slowly as possible, in tongues and in English, singing, standing, sitting, lying, running. Every possible permutation of different methods of prayer. Finally that morning when I couldn't handle it anymore and got outside the door… I had been there twenty-five minutes. I thought that was progress but it was going to be a long time before I could sit on a hill for days as Elijah had done! I certainly hadn't gone hungry like Peter!

I kept going down to the chapel each Saturday morning. It was hard work but I persevered because I thought that if these other people can do it then I could do it too. I wanted to be a man of God and I would do whatever it took to become a man of God.

Then one day something happened. As I was praying, suddenly the presence of the Lord came into the room. I had felt His presence many, many times before but I had never felt it at this level when I was alone by myself. I had experienced a powerful sense of God's presence with others in a meeting but never on my own. This was quite amazing. When His presence came, my immediate thought was that I should not do anything that would cause it to leave the room. I had my Bible in my hand and I was very hesitant to open it. I didn't ask for anything that I thought might be construed as being self-centered or having a wrong motive. I just stood there before Him and only did what felt totally comfortable with His presence. After a while His presence was gone, dissipating like mist off a mountainside. Suddenly I realized that I was there by myself. He had gone. I looked at my watch. Over an hour had gone by and it seemed like five minutes. I didn't realize it then but I was learning the secret not only of prayer, but the secret of the Christian life.

The whole of Christian life is really focused on one thing. That one thing is to find His presence and stay there, to learn to live with a conscious reality of His presence with you. Each time I went down on to the chapel after that day I would be looking for His presence. Sometimes it came, sometimes it didn't, but it came more and more regularly. I was learning how to find His presence more and more.

Then one day as I was praying something happened that changed everything. It was the last time I ever went there. His presence came and I was with Him. By now my prayer times were getting to three or four hours. I was pacing around the chapel with my Bible opened in my hand. As I reached the wall and turned round, suddenly the Lord spoke to me.

That moment has affected what I am today. Beyond that, and unknown to me at the time, it has affected the lives of thousands. He spoke to me in an extremely challenging way. He asked a question that shook me to the core. The question contained five words but there was so much packed into it. Remember that I was struggling with all the questions about receiving the Father's love. He spoke with perfect communication, His presence becoming what I can only describe as being highly intentional. Suddenly I was under the spotlight. I felt like He was watching intently to see how I would respond to His question.

Somehow I knew that He could see what I was thinking and feeling. Every response within me was laid bare. I was scared as I was put under the scrutiny of the Lord. It felt like a searchlight combined with an x-ray. Hebrews 4:13 says, *"All things are naked and laid bare before the eyes of Him with whom we have to do."* The scary thing for me was that I became aware of the reality of this. I was exposed under His unrelenting gaze. I stood there trying to work out how to answer this question. It was very simple to understand but very hard to deal with.

He simply said to me, *"James, whose son are you?"*

If He had asked a slightly different question, or if He had put it a different way, I could have answered it easily. If He had said to me, "James, who is your father?" I could have said to Him, "Bruce Jordan is my father." There is no doubt about it. Bruce Jordan *is* my father. And I would have simply answered, "It's Bruce. Bruce Jordan is my father!" But He didn't ask me who my father was - He asked me *whose son* I was. And I realized when He asked that question, that a long, long time before, I *had stopped* being a son to my father.

CLOSING MY HEART TO MY DAD

I remember clearly, when I was about ten years old, sitting in a barber's chair getting a haircut. I was sitting with my arms on the arms of the old leather barber's chair. Everyone in our town had at least one rifle for hunting and for participating in the shooting competitions, which took place on a regular basis. The barber was the most renowned hunter in the town. He would go off into the hills with nothing more than his rifle and a blanket to sleep in, a bag of flour with some rice and some salt for food, and he would be gone for weeks. My mother, however, was the best shot in town. She was a real "Annie Oakley." She would go out rabbit shooting and come back with sixty to ninety rabbits in an afternoon and all of them shot right through the head. I still have her rifle today.

While he was cutting my hair, another man came in and was chatting to him. "How was your recent deer hunting trip?" the barber enquired. The man then said something that changed my life. He commented that his hunting trip had been unsuccessful because the government deer cullers had been through and left few deer to hunt. These deer cullers were employed by the government to live in the mountains and shoot the deer. That was all they did, staying in the huts and sleeping under rocks. When I heard this, I immediately understood that these government cullers were better hunters than the best hunter in town because they had shot all the deer and left none for the other hunters. From that moment on, all I wanted was to live alone in the hills and shoot deer for the government.

I love mountains, but what really drew me was the sense of freedom from relationships that this lifestyle promised. I had discovered that people could hurt me and I thought that, if I could live without people, I could live without pain. Most of my pain was in connection with my father. When I heard about the government deer cullers I basically gave up making any effort at school. Every time I got a report card my teachers said to my parents, "James has the highest capacity in the classroom, but he doesn't use it." I could get by and pass all the exams without having to be at school very much. Because of this I would spend as much time as possible outside of school. I was just putting in the time until I was eighteen, and old enough to become a deer culler. In fact, they let me start when I was seventeen. I had been so hurt by my father that I had closed my heart to him before I was ten years old, and I had not been a son to him from that point on.

Now, when the Lord faced me with that question, "James, whose son are you?" I knew immediately that He was looking for a name. The question was extremely specific. "James, *whose son are you? Give Me a name!*"

The first thing I thought to say to Him was, "I am Bruce Jordan's son." Immediately though, I realized that I couldn't say that because He was watching my heart and He knew that I had not been a son to my father.

The question stirred up some deep stuff within me. Over the previous few months I had been reading the book of John and had been impacted by what Jesus said about His relationship with His Father. I had underlined every statement that He made. Statements such as, *"I delight to do Thy will,"* or, *"I have food to eat that you do not know of. It is my food to do the will of my Father and to finish His work."* I suddenly realized that doing His Father's will was such a satisfying thing for Jesus that sometimes He didn't even feel physical hunger. And when I looked at my own relationship with my father, I began to see that it was totally different. I understood that what the Lord was really saying to me was, "James, to whom have you been a son, like Jesus is a son to Me?" That was what He was really asking.

The Lord was putting His finger on a major issue in the preparation of my heart to receive the Father's love. My attitude to my earthly father was a massive blockage within my heart to receiving the fatherhood of God.

MY DAD

One of my abiding memories of my dad was that he had a real capacity for making arguments especially when he was drunk, which was often. No matter what one said, he would take the other side and provoke and be contentious. When I was a little boy I didn't understand that my father had problems that he was locked into. I just thought that he hated me. He used to provoke me to the point where I would literally lose control of my body and go berserk with anger and frustration. When he would provoke an argument, all I heard him saying was that I was stupid. *"There's something wrong with your brain. You're an idiot. You're not good enough for me. I don't like you. You're crazy. You can't think straight. There's something wrong with you!"* Since then I've learned something about arguments. Arguing has nothing to do with the subject. The subject is merely a tool, which an argumentative person employs to give them the upper hand. An argument is actually a power struggle.

Doubtless my father had some issues. So did I, but I was just a little boy. And when he would use all the strength of an adult voice, an adult mind, and all the power of his personality against me, there were times when I actually kicked cupboard doors off their hinges. I would almost literally see red, slam the door, and run to the hill behind our house, fuming and crying until my heart would settle down. I would come back when all the lights were out, climb in my bedroom window and go to sleep. No one came to check whether or not I came back. There would be tension in the house for days. Then slowly it would dissipate until the next argument. Growing up with that I closed my heart to my father.

FORGIVING FROM YOUR WILL

Shortly after I became a Christian a man came to preach in our church. The message he preached was basically this, *"You must forgive others who have sinned against you. If you do not forgive, God will not forgive you."* I understood what he was saying. I had read the Scriptures many times. But I interpreted it as an issue of eternal security. By not forgiving you could lose your salvation. I couldn't really think of any alternative meanings of that verse.

If there is one subject that I am hot on, this is it! I believe many, many Christians across the world have been deceived about what *forgiveness* actually is. Many Christians think that they have forgiven someone, when in their heart they really haven't. They believe that the issue is dealt with because they have forgiven in the way that they have been taught. As I listened to this preacher I felt under immense pressure to forgive my father, or I would lose my salvation. I was trapped! I wanted to leave the room but I couldn't. I thought that if I left the room I would be walking out of Christianity. So I stayed there and the pressure got worse and worse.

The harsh reality was that I did not want to forgive my father. I didn't have a bone in my body that was remotely interested in forgiving him. But the preacher was adamant that I had to.

IT'S NOT ABOUT THE WILL

Finally, at the end of the meeting, he said, "Anyone who needs to forgive someone come forward now." So I went forward, still battling within myself, and one of the elders came and stood beside me. Finally, after a long time not being able to bring myself to say the words to forgive my Dad, he said to me, "James, use your will."

When he said that, I knew it was the key for me to be able to get out of the room, because I knew how to use my will. There were times when I had been in the mountains when bad weather struck, and the rivers flooded and I would be drenched and cold. In that situation, if you don't get to a distant hut by nightfall, you are probably not going to survive the night. So you engage your will and make it through the wind and rain to the hut. Those sorts of situations are very real, so I knew what it was to put my will into action. So, when this elder said this, I shut off the emotions and, with an act of will, said, "I forgive my father in Jesus' name." I was so relieved. The tears stopped. I was happy. I felt that my eternal salvation was secure.

Back in the chapel that day, when the Lord asked me whose son I was, I realized that I still had huge issues about my father in my heart. I had not been a son to him. I had not related to him. I didn't even want to relate to him. The arguments between him and I were still going from time to time. I didn't realize until that day that my earlier profession of forgiveness was nothing more than a veneer.

Many people have been led to believe that forgiveness is a choice. It may well start with a choice but that is not really what forgiveness is. The words, "I forgive you" spoken merely as an act of the will do not amount to genuine forgiveness.

Let me pause telling my story about what happened in the chapel until the next chapter and get into the essence of what I wish to communicate in this chapter.

FORGIVING BY THE WILL
VERSUS FORGIVING FROM THE HEART

Many people believe they have forgiven simply because they have made a choice, they have used their will and they have said the words of forgiveness.

The word "forgiveness" has become such a cliché that most Christians assume blithely that they know what forgiveness is. What I wish to say here through this writing is quite different. In fact, I have never heard any other preacher say what I am going to say.

Come with me to Matthew Chapter 18. The first part of the story starts in verse 21, when Peter came and asked Jesus a question about forgiveness. It says, *"Then Peter came up and said to him, 'Lord, how often will my brother sin against me, and I forgive him? As many as seven times?'"*

That was Peter's question. He was really saying, "Lord, how far does this forgiveness issue actually go? How many times must I do it?"

I detect reluctance in Peter in the way that he put the question. More than likely, Peter had witnessed the grace and mercy that was in Jesus towards the woman who was caught in adultery and in many other incidents that happened. When the man was lowered through the roof to be healed, Jesus' first words to him were, *"Son, your sins have been forgiven you,"* and the man hadn't even asked for forgiveness! Peter had witnessed Jesus forgiving sins and extending mercy in a very free and generous manner. He would have watched this over a period of time thinking, "Jesus, to what extent does this go? How do you reconcile forgiveness with the demands of the Law?" As Peter posed this incredible question, he exposed his heart. Jesus' reply to him was, *"I do not say to you up to seven times, but up to seventy times seven."*

I don't believe for one minute that Jesus meant to forgive exactly four-hundred and ninety times and beyond that Peter was off the hook. Jesus was really saying that forgiveness is endless. He exposed the fact that Peter was clueless about what forgiveness really is.

As forgiveness is generally understood today, it would follow that to forgive the same person for the same sin seven times would be extremely difficult. When someone sins against you it always hurts. There is always pain involved in one way or another. So to forgive them and cancel that and let them off repeatedly would hurt more and more each time. Mostly we would call the person to account after the second or third time and the friendship would be lost. So when Peter said, "Lord, seven times?" he thought he was being very godly. In reality, however, it showed that he completely misunderstood it. The grace, mercy and forgiveness that Jesus was talking about were in an entirely different dimension.

LOVING MERCY

To show what Jesus meant let us look at Micah 6:8. Many people have wall plaques quoting this verse.

"He has shown you, oh man what is good; and what does the Lord require of you: To do justly, and to love mercy, and to walk humbly with your God."

To love mercy!! Mercy is a heart to see the guilty go free.

It is forgiveness. God's desire is that we would *love* forgiving. It is not to be something that you must do, but it is something that you *love* to do. The kind of heart that God wants is a heart that *loves* to forgive.

If you love something, you will do it endlessly. You will do it every time you get the opportunity. What is more, you will be looking for opportunities to do it. When Peter asked, "Lord, how many times must I forgive my brother, when he sins against me?" what he was really saying was, "This is *hard work*. I don't like doing this, I find it difficult. I don't want to forgive." But *Jesus'* reply was, "Peter, you have no idea what forgiveness really is."

Jesus went on to tell a story to help Peter understand the difference. We have often missed that point. Peter didn't really understand what forgiveness was. He thought it was done by human determination against what a person *really* wanted to do. I have often talked to people who have said to me, "Someone did this to me and I imagine that I'm going to have to forgive them every day of my life." Yes, there is a process of forgiveness. It took me six months to get through this with my father. I am not saying that there isn't a process, because there certainly is. The Lord began to take me through these next verses in Matthew so that I could come to forgive my father in the way that He wanted me to. He wants us to progress from choosing to forgive, to forgiving with love, and then to the place where we *love* to forgive. Moving far beyond forgiving as an act of the will, to forgiving endlessly from a heart that *loves* to forgive.

Most of the church today has been taught that forgiveness is an issue of choice and an act of the will. Jesus disagrees. He says that forgiveness is an issue of the heart.

FORGIVENESS IS CANCELING A DEBT

In this passage, Jesus, realizing that Peter saw forgiveness only as a hard command that must be obeyed, told a story to explain and to lead Peter into a forgiveness that he would love and that would come from his heart. Let me paraphrase the story.

There was a king who had a servant who embezzled a tremendous amount of money out of the kingdom. Whether he gambled it, made poor investments or spent it all, it was gone. When he was discovered, he begged the king to forgive him. The king forgave him and cancelled the debt.

This servant then went out and in a short space of time met someone who owed him a small amount of money. The man also begged to be forgiven for the small amount of money but the one who was forgiven the huge amount would not forgive this person and had him thrown him in jail until he paid it back. This got back to the king who called the servant back in and said to him, "I forgave you all that, and you didn't forgive somebody a small amount!" Because of that the king threw him into jail, where he was tortured and in torment.

That is the story. In verse 34 it says, *"And in anger his master delivered him to the tormentors, until he should pay all his debt."* Then Jesus uttered what is probably one of the most serious comments in the New Testament, *"So also my heavenly Father will do to every one of you, if you do not forgive your brother from your heart."* In other words, you will be in torment until you forgive from your heart. Jesus told the story for one purpose. To teach us how to really forgive from our hearts.

We must ultimately come to this place where we *forgive from the heart*. The truth is, *your will is not your heart*. Your will is yours. Your heart is *you*. We know this because a person can control the will. You can determine to set your will to do something or *not* to do something. Many people, who have made a choice to forgive but have not forgiven from their heart are still living in some form of torment, thinking, *"This can't be anything to do with forgiveness because I have already forgiven. I've made the choice, so for me, forgiveness is over. The problems that are in my life right now cannot be anything to do with forgiveness, because I have forgiven, as I've been taught to."* In fact, forgiveness *is* still the issue, but they cannot face it because they believe that it has been completed in their life.

So let us come back to the story, which the Lord took me through verse by verse to help me forgive my Dad. Jesus said,

"Therefore the kingdom of heaven may be compared to a king who wished to settle accounts with his servants."

When I read that verse, the Lord spoke very clearly and simply to me, *"James, as you read the story put yourself in the place of the king."* This king has to forgive someone, so to understand how it works for us we need to put ourselves in the position of the king.

As I put myself in the place of the king, my father became the servant who had stolen so much from me. This king decided, for reasons unknown, to have all of the accounts of his kingdom settled and made right. Anything that was wrong, he wanted it to be put right. He wanted all of the hidden things to be uncovered and put right. It became his determination to have a kingdom that was righteous.

As you are reading this you can put yourself in the place of the king. You can say, "Lord, I want all the accounts of my life to be put right. If there are things that are not really forgiven, then show me what they are. If I have deceived myself or if I've not been able to see, Lord, would You bring that to my attention so that here, today, we can begin to face it? Lord, I want the accounts of my kingdom to be settled."

The story continues, "*When he began to settle, one was brought to him who owed him ten thousand talents.*" This was roughly equivalent to one hundred million US dollars in today's currency! This servant was obviously a trusted man, holding a position of influence in the kingdom.

The worst sins, the ones that wound us the most, are usually from people who are close to us and that we have trusted. Generally, when you don't trust someone, what they do against you just confirms what you expected, but when you trust them it inflicts a more grievous wound. This man had a place close to the king's heart. He was trusted and he was found to be stealing money from his master.

This is why when someone sins against you it hurts. Because when they sin against you they are always taking something from your life. You are being stolen from.

You don't have to be in ministry very long until you discover that some people have been sinned against in horrendous ways. The damage to their lives because of what someone else has done can be absolutely devastating. When somebody sins against you they are always stealing something from your life.

Denise and I were ministering to a lady once in Minnesota who was eighty-three years old. When she was a three year-old child, she had been raped. She didn't think that it had any relation to what she came to talk to us about. Her problem was the fact that she had been married five times and each one of her husbands had divorced her. She was broken-hearted about these men whom she had loved who had all rejected her. They had all said the same thing, namely that she was unable to be affectionate as a wife, and so they rejected her. As we heard her story we discovered that she had been raped when she was three years old. She couldn't see what was increasingly obvious to us. That her marital problems were a matter of cause and effect and that she was living with the legacy of her childhood abuse.

What happened to her when she was three years old destroyed something of her femininity, of her womanhood. It took away her capacity to be able to relate freely in a loving way, and to enjoy intimacy of relationship. That was stolen from her. Later, I realized that what had been stolen from her was not only her womanhood, but much more besides. The experience of having a happy marriage and children was stolen from her. The chance of her ever becoming a grandmother was stolen from her. All of the benefits that a stable marriage would produce over a lifetime were stolen from her. As a woman of eighty-three she had none of those things. They were stolen from her when she was a three year-old child.

I put my arms around her and asked that the Father would come and pour His love into that three year-old part of her heart and heal that wound. A miracle happened that day. This elderly woman suddenly began giggling like a three year-old girl. She was giggling uncontrollably with joy. Then she stopped and looked at us with a very serious expression and she said, "Why did it take God so long to heal me?" I had no answer to that question. All I could think to say to her was, "Well, better late than never, I guess." Hearing that, immediately she began giggling again, "Yes! Better late than never!" It was a real joy for her to hear that. She was healed.

When people sin against us the fact is that they are *always* stealing something from us.

If we don't understand what is stolen, we cannot cancel the debt.

Many people make a very quick and shallow apology when they have done something wrong, "Brother, I'm sorry. Please forgive me." We know that is the Christian thing to ask! And the Christian response is, "Yes, I forgive you", and we think that it is over. But actually, in most cases, the relationship never got healed. There is no restoration of relationship but because we uttered the words of forgiveness we cannot identify what is wrong. There are a lot of superficial relationships in the body of Christ for this very reason. Wounds of the heart that have never been healed. *If we don't understand what is stolen, we cannot cancel the debt.*

So in this story, ten thousand talents were stolen. For this king to forgive, he has to cancel the debt equivalent to one hundred million dollars. That is a lot of money.

HEART FORGIVENESS WILL COST YOU

Let me use this little scenario. Imagine that one day I walk past your place, and decide to drop by and borrow $20 from you. When I arrive at your house you are not home but the door is open and I can see your wallet on the table. I take a look and I think to myself, "If he was here he would give me that. He's my friend. So I'll just take it anyway." So I go in and take the $20 and spend it, and it's all gone.

When you come home later, you notice immediately that the $20 is missing. You are thinking, "Someone has stolen that! I shouldn't have left the door open." However, the next day the Holy Spirit convicts me and I realize that I have sinned. This wasn't a loan. I have actually stolen this. So I come back to you and say, "Brother, I'm so sorry, but yesterday, when you were out, I came into your house and I took $20 out of your wallet and I've spent it and it's gone. Will you forgive me?"

You now have a choice, but the choice is going to have an emotional issue attached to it because you are probably emotionally connected to that $20. To let that $20 go you must cancel the debt. If you don't forgive me then I have to pay it back. Unforgiveness demands the sinner to make full restitution. *Forgiveness cancels the debt.* The one thing about forgiveness that makes it difficult for us is the fact that the innocent pay for the guilty. It has always been this way. We see it in Jesus. His forgiveness of sinners cost Him His life! Forgiveness and mercy actually go against justice. It's going to cost you $20 to forgive me.

The wonderful thing about forgiveness is this: when we forgive somebody, it makes us more like Jesus. When we cancel a debt, when we are paying for another person's sin, then it connects us more closely and changes us to become more like Him.

So you may think, "What is $20 between James and I? He's not such a bad guy. He made a mistake here. Ok, I cancel the debt." So you say, "Ok, I forgive you." I go away and I'm free and will never have to pay the debt.

Now, let me just change this story a bit. When I go into your house and open your wallet to take the $20 out, I notice your VISA card there. What is more, you have accidently left the PIN number in the back. So I take the VISA card and the $20 note, and I go down to the bank and I withdraw $1000 out of your bank account, and return the VISA card back to your wallet. I take the $20 as well and I spend it all. $1020. It's all gone. The next day I'm convicted. However, when you come home and the VISA card is still in your wallet, you only miss the $20. You won't know about the missing $1000 until a later time when you check your statement.

The next day when the Holy Spirit convicts me and I come and say to you, "Brother, I'm so sorry but yesterday I stole some money from you. Will you forgive me?" Notice that I don't give the details about taking the VISA card so you think that it is only $20. In reality, I stole $1020 but I'm asking you to forgive me for all that I took from you. So when I say to you, "Brother, I stole some money from you. Will you forgive me?" and you say, "What's $20 between James and I? Ok James, I forgive you."

Let me ask the question. Am I forgiven? No! I am *not* forgiven.

You can't forgive me unless you know what has been taken! You have forgiven me for the $20 but when you get your VISA statement, you're going to have to go through the whole process again. And you will be much more emotional about $1000 than about $20. This is going to touch your life in a very real way. Maybe that $1000 was reserved for your holiday or something quite important to you. $1000 is not a small amount. And so in your heart, it's a bigger issue to forgive me for that.

You see, for many of us, when we forgave somebody for something, we have never really looked at what was stolen.

I was discovering this when the Lord was taking me through forgiveness with my father. I had said at the front of the church with that elder, "I forgive my father in Jesus' name" and so much pain had come to the surface in my life while I was trying to say the words. But, now as I was reading these verses, the Lord began to bring back to my mind an awareness of what my father's inability to be the father I needed had cost me.

I began to realize that if my father could have just said to me, in the middle of an argument, "Son, I don't want to argue with you, I love you. You're a good boy. You've got a good mind. I like you. You're my son." That would have made a big difference. But he kept taunting and taunting, until I would lose my temper.

Sometimes I look at old family photographs of the time when I was a teenager. In each photograph without exception my face was turned away from my father. When I look at my face in those old photographs I feel like weeping. I was a poor, broken kid. If my father could have simply put his hand on my shoulder as he passed by it would have made a huge difference to my life. If he could have told me that he loved me. If he only would have sat down and just said to me, "Son, how is your day going?" My father was not a bad father, but he was extremely damaged by the Second World War. If he could have been a better father, my life would have been a better life. My father was never physically violent but his words were constantly cruel and cutting. I began to get in touch with what it had cost me that my father was the man that he was. And I began to get really, really angry.

MY FATHER COULD NOT PAY

As God was taking me through this process of counting the cost, there were times when I wanted to get on a plane and fly back home. Sometimes I felt so angry that I wanted to punch my father. I was shocked at how much anger was lurking deep inside my heart. I felt so broken. I was starting to get in touch with the real cost of my father's inability to be the father that I needed.

Keeping with the story in Matthew 18 - in verse 25 it says, *"And since he could not pay* (this is the man who had stolen ten thousand talents), *his master ordered him to be sold, with his wife and children, and all that he had, and payment to be made."* I wanted my father to be punished. Unforgiveness wants the other person to pay for what they did. But the words that stuck out to me were the first words of the verse, *"Since he could not pay."* This man had stolen a massive sum of money and it was all gone. He could not give it back.

As the weeks went on, those words kept coming back to me, *"Since he could not pay."* And the Lord started to remind me of things that I had heard about my father. People he was in the war with, my uncles and aunts. I began to see his life in a different way. I remembered the way that my aunts (his sisters) talked about him with a sneering tone in their voice. My father had to leave home when he was 16. He was sent to a city a great distance away in those days, and allowed to return home only once a year. He lived with an elderly lady in a house close to where he worked, doing a job he hated with nothing at home to interest him at all. On his annual return home his mother would greet him with a handshake and say goodbye a week later with a handshake. He told me some years later that the only person who ever said, "I love you" to him was my mother.

When he was seventeen, the Second World War started. He joined the Territorial Army immediately to get trained and was sent off to fight in the Pacific Islands. Then he went to Egypt and was part of the Allied advance through Italy, where he remained until the end of the war. He recounted once how he witnessed his closest friend being killed by a direct hit from a tank shell. I remember him saying, "We never found even a scrap of his clothing." He was a spotter for the heavy artillery, locating enemy positions and calling in artillery fire, directing shells onto the target. Mostly they never saw where they had fired except once when they travelled through a village that had been obliterated. He saw bits of the bodies of the women and children in the streets. There were no men or enemy soldiers there - only women and children! My father was nineteen and he was the one who had directed the shells onto the village.

I often look back and I think that if I was God that day, and could have seen my father's heart when they went through that village, how would I have felt towards him? I think I would have felt anger towards what had happened, and sorrow towards him, seeing what his hands had done and what he had been a part of. My father came back from the war needing to be loved. He got married very quickly to my mother and within a few years they had three children. He began to drink as much alcohol as he could because he couldn't handle the emotions and the memories that haunted him. My father had an argument with the world within him because of the injustice of his life. Consequently he turned everything into an argument because there was a deep dissatisfaction within him. He had three children who needed a father to love them. But he didn't have any love to give!

Reading those words, *"Since he could not pay,"* I realized that my father had no capacity left in him to be a father. He didn't have love to give. He couldn't pay what he owed me.

You cannot give what you don't have

You see, you cannot give what you haven't received – and yet sometimes we can think things are so simple, "Why can't they do that? It's so simple." But if you have never received it, it is not as simple. My father had never heard anyone say to him, "I love you." He never had a father put his hand on his shoulder and say, "I'm proud of you, son." All he had in his heart was an argument with the world. *He was not able to pay.* I began to see my father as simply another human being who had suffered, who was imperfect and who, like me, couldn't handle much of what life had thrown at him.

"Then the master of that servant was moved with compassion, released him and forgave him the debt." (v27).

The master was *moved with compassion*. When I saw that my father simply didn't have the means to pay me, for the first time in my life I had compassion for my father. I had never thought about things from his perspective. I think if I could have had God's perspective and seen all of the things that had happened in my father's life, I would have had a very different attitude towards him.

The real thief

We have an enemy of our souls. This enemy comes to steal, kill and destroy. But he doesn't come to steal your car. He comes to steal your soul. He doesn't come to destroy your TV set or something. He comes to destroy your personality. He comes to kill everything good in you, everything godly, everything kind, everything pleasant and everything gentle. He comes to destroy everything that has any hint of God in it.

As Christians, we have a shield of faith to deflect the fiery darts of the enemy. I realized that my father never even had a shield, and so all the fiery darts of the enemy hit him. Satan is totally unscrupulous. He does not hold back in any way, does not exert any control on the evil that he will do to any person. He will do the most horrendous things to the most pure and innocent little child. He had been attacking my father from the moment my father was born, even prior to his birth. Everyone who has ever hurt you, he has been attacking too. He has been attacking and destroying your father and mother in ways that you will never understand. Stealing from them their potential to be the people that they dreamed they would be, to incapacitate them from being the parents that you needed.

So I began to understand something of my father's life and began to see that he was just a man like me. Battling with the problems of this world, trying to do the best he could, he just didn't have the capacity to be what I needed him to be. For the first time in my life, I had compassion for him. For the first time in my life, I prayed for my father. And I prayed something like this,

"Lord, I want my father to be blessed. I want him to be happy. I don't want him to carry this guilt anymore. I don't want him to lack being loved. I don't want him to be alone anymore. I want him to be loved. I want him to be forgiven for the things in his conscience and all the things from the war that disturbed him. I don't want him to have to carry that in him anymore. All of the things that caused him to drink so much that he was trying to stifle his heart. Lord, I'm asking You to forgive him for all those things so that he can lay it down and leave it behind and be free. Lord, would You forgive him for his sins, could You forgive him for everything? I don't even want him to feel guilty for the way he mis-fathered me anymore, because

that is just adding to all of the other problems of his life. I want him to be free of the feelings of failure as a man, as a father, as a husband. I want him to be free! Lord, I want him to be blessed. Lord, I forgive him with all my heart. Would You forgive him?"

When I prayed that prayer I realized that I genuinely wanted him to be forgiven for *his* sake. He was carrying so much stuff and *I wanted him to be free.* I can tell you this – with that kind of forgiveness, you *will love* forgiving. When I said, "Lord, I forgive him with all my heart" a funny thing happened that I didn't expect.

Suddenly I felt incredibly empty. In my heart I felt so alone and vulnerable. I felt like a little child who was totally unprotected. When you don't forgive from the heart you are holding onto the person who owes you the debt. When you let them go, you are empty.

I forgave my father and cancelled the debt. I released him from all of his obligations as a father, from being what he could never be. I stopped expecting things from him because that was just another weight on his shoulders. I released him from my hope that he would make it up to me one day. Suddenly, I felt completely empty and totally alone. I felt like a little boy with no one to protect me.

In that moment, as the feeling hit me, I suddenly had a strange vision. In the vision I was a schoolteacher in a classroom of approximately thirty kids. I yelled at these twelve year-old kids, "Who will be a father to me?" The children looked at me perplexed. They were only kids. How could they parent me? I yelled it again and again, "Who will be a father to me?" but of course they didn't know what to say. Then I noticed right behind them at the back of the class, a hand went up. As I looked over the top of all the heads, sitting on the floor in the back of the class leaning against the wall was our heavenly Father. And He said, "James, I will be a father to you."

Heart forgiveness is when your heart releases the person, frees them, and lets them go. When your heart is connected to somebody in unforgiveness it is not free to be connected to your heavenly Father. God wants to know us heart to heart, as a father. When we release our mother or our father from our hearts, then our hearts are free to be connected to our heavenly Father who says, "I will receive you and I will be a father to you… and you shall be my sons and daughters." (2 Corinthians 6:17-18.) You have a heavenly Father who wants to know you deeply and intimately. You may still be bound to your parents in unforgiveness. It is time to forgive from the heart and let them go.

CHAPTER 4

The Heart of Sonship

~

I now want to finish telling you what happened in the chapel that morning. This was hugely significant in bringing me into the experience of the Father's love.

When the Lord posed that shattering question, "James, whose son are you?" it was a most incredible communication. I knew that He was asking, "To whom have you been a son, like Jesus is a son to Me?" There was so much more also involved in this issue that I stood for a long time trying to find an answer. I was stunned at the Lord's question to me, trying to work out how to answer that question. There were two issues going around in my mind at the same time, like two discs spinning crazily in opposite directions, I was going through everything that I could think of, trying to get one answer that would satisfy both issues. What would I say? It was a very intense moment and I knew that the Lord was able to see and was watching the inner workings of my heart, mind and feelings. Like a searchlight, He was looking inside me to see my reactions to His question.

The first thing that came to my mind in response to, "James, whose son are you?" was to come up with a name, and the first name that I came up with was my father's name. I thought that I could just say to the Lord, "I am Bruce Jordan's son," but as soon as that thought came to my mind, I realized that I couldn't say that to the Lord, because I had stopped being a son to my father a long time before. Of course I was his son by birth, but I was not a son to him like Jesus was a son to His Father. So I had to wipe that from my mind and quickly come up with another answer.

The next person who came to my mind was an elder in the church where we got saved. He was a remarkable man. His name was Ken Wright. He had been walking in the Spirit for many years. He also was the man who had baptized me. I remember seeing his itinerary one time for a two-year ministry trip around the world. He was not going to be in any one place for more than four days, in the whole two years, and he visited more than one hundred different countries. When he would speak, we would drink in his words and the Spirit in him would flow over us. We were very impressed with him and he had something of a father's heart towards us.

So when the Lord posed the question, "James, whose son are you?" it suddenly came to my mind that I could say that I was Ken Wright's son but again, the moment that thought occurred to me, I knew I couldn't say it, because (although I had gleaned everything that I could from Ken) I certainly didn't have a son's heart towards him. Jesus said to His Father, "I delight to do Your will" but I had never desired to please Ken. I took everything that he gave that would please me. So I realized, "I can't say that to the Lord either. Who else can I say? I can't say Bruce Jordan. I can't say Ken Wright, so who can I say that I have been a son to?"

The only other man I could think of was Neville Winger. We used to call him "Uncle Nev." Uncle Nev owned a successful car sales business in New Zealand and sold it all to purchase a farm on an island off the coast of New Zealand. It was a run-down old farm, set in eight hundred acres of hill country with a beautiful but rugged coastline. He moved out there with his wife Dot, and for many years they had been taking troubled street kids into their home. Nev and Dot had a heart for young people and they would bring them into their home and try to work with them. So he was looking for a place where he could bring these kids off the street and care for them in his own home. He also wanted a conference centre and a revival centre for New Zealand and he bought this farm for the purpose of fulfilling his vision.

Nev was an extraordinary man, a true spiritual father in the nation. When he preached I really connected with him and thought that I would like to attend the Bible school that he had started; which we did. Somehow Nev, like Ken, had something of the heart of a father towards us. He prophesied over us at length and all these years later it is still relevant.

So I thought that I would say to the Lord, "I'm Nev Winger's son," but *again*, being under God's searchlight, I realized that I couldn't say that. The truth was that I had never been a son to him in my heart. I had been a taker, not a giver. A true son, as Jesus was, is always concerned with his father's business. I was never concerned with my father's business *or* Ken Wright's business *or* Nev Winger's business. I never ever considered how to be a blessing or a help to these men. I had a totally orphaned heart. I was squirming and wrestling when I should have simply said, "Lord, I am nobody's son and I *don't want* to be anybody's son." I couldn't admit that because there was something else going on.

When I had closed my heart to my father I had lost the heart of a son completely.

The Spirit of Sonship

What is the heart of sonship? To understand this let us begin at Galatians 4:4, which says,

"When the fullness of time had come, God sent forth His Son, born of a woman, born under the law, to redeem those who were under the law, that we might receive the adoption as sons."

When we are born again, we become sons and daughters of God by adoption. God, however, goes further than adoption. Adoption is only the first step. Paul continues,

"Because you are sons, God sent forth the Spirit of His Son into your hearts crying, 'Abba! Father!'"

Because you are God's son by legal right, He has poured forth the Spirit of His Son. He has put that spirit into our hearts, the Spirit that cries, *"Abba! Father!"* An adopted child doesn't cry "Abba! Father!" Our human hearts don't cry "Abba! Father!" It is the Spirit of the Son in us, which cries, "Abba! Father!"

The Spirit of His Son is poured into our hearts. When I closed my heart to my father, I lost the heart of a son. So when the Holy Spirit was poured into me there was no corresponding heart of sonship. Because I had closed my heart as a son, the Holy Spirit was unable to bring forth sonship within me. This is a vital point, which the Lord was exposing to me when He posed that question. He was looking for a heart that was open to sonship.

Jesus experienced this when the Holy Spirit descended upon Him at His baptism. When God announced, *"This is My beloved Son, in whom I am well pleased,"* the Spirit of sonship descended on Him. From that point on Jesus was proclaimed to the whole world to be the Son of God! Prior to that, He was Jesus of Nazareth, the son of Joseph and Mary, but now He is proclaimed to be the Son of God. The same Holy Spirit that fell on Jesus is the same Spirit that creates sonship in us.

Many Christians have known the Holy Spirit as the Spirit of adoption but have yet to experience Him as the Spirit of sonship. Consequently, we can be filled with the Holy Spirit and have no life of sonship at all. When the Spirit gets poured into the heart of a person who has no heart of sonship to their own parents, then the Holy Spirit cannot function in that person as the Spirit of a son. *The Spirit of God has to find a corresponding harmony within you for it to be made real in your life experience.*

When I closed my heart to my father, I lost the heart of a son. When I closed my heart to my father, I no longer had the heart of a son towards any father figures... including God.

RELATING TO A FATHER

This was my big problem. There were lots of people who came into my life who had something of a heart of a father towards me but I had no way of relating to that. I didn't realize that if you don't have the heart of a son towards your natural mother and father then you don't have the heart of a son at all, and therefore you cannot make a connection with any father *including* God the Father! In the same way that making Jesus absolute Lord is a prerequisite for having a relationship with Him, having the heart of a son or daughter is crucial to having a relationship with God the Father.

If you want to know God the Father, there is only one way that you can know Him. He is not going to relate to you as anything other than Father. Many of us have become fathers at some point in our lives, but God never *became* Father, He *always* was Father and He always will be Father. He created the universe, but He is not creator by nature. Creating is something that He does, not who He is in His essential nature. If your father is an engineer, for example, you don't relate to him on the basis of his occupation, you relate to him on the basis of his identity in the relationship. God created the universe but He doesn't relate to you as a creator. He relates to you as a Father because that is who He is. Father is the very essence of His being. Jesus came to reveal that Yahweh is Papa, that Yahweh *is* Father.

I believe that probably more than ninety percent of us in the Western world have closed our hearts to our parents. We have used sophisticated language about it but the reality of intimate relationship is something that is very foreign to the experience of many people

So when I was in that chapel and the Lord spoke those words to me, "James, whose son are you?" what He was really getting at was the state of my heart. I was lost for answers. I should have said, "Lord, I'm nobody's son." but I had a problem saying that. Let me tell you why.

ALL THE MEN OF GOD ARE SOMEBODY'S SON

As long as I had been a Christian I wanted to be a man of God, just like the anointed preachers. I was continually praying, "Lord, make me into a man of God." When I was in the chapel that day, trying to come up with a name that I could say to the Lord, another thought process was spinning in my head. It was related to a favourite subject of mine at the time. While I was at Bible School I had done a major study project on the chronology of the Old Testament. As I was researching the famous characters of the Old Testament something continually irked me. Almost all of these heroes were described as being "the son of..." Joshua was the son of Nun, Caleb was the son of Jephunneh, David was the son of Jesse. Every person that I read about was described in terms of being the son of another.

This really annoyed me. Why not David the poet, the warrior-king? Why not Isaiah the great prophet? Why not Caleb the man of faith? I was so self-reliant that I thought, "Why can't these guys stand on their own two feet? Why can't they be real men? Why do they need a daddy to lean on?" This revealed the true state of my own heart in relation to my father.

That day in the chapel I felt that God was saying, "James, I have heard you asking Me to make you into a man of God. Do you want to be a man of God? Is that right? Well, *all* of My men are somebody's son. So if you want to be a man of God, James, whose son are you?"

JESUS WAS THE SON OF AN IMPERFECT MAN

I *knew* the harm that fathers could cause. Didn't these biblical heroes know the harm that fathers cause? You must be crazy to be a son to someone! I knew that Jesus is the Son of God but I could forgive Him for that because His Father is perfect. Perfect fathers are not the problem; imperfect fathers are the problem! Then I realized that Jesus is known eternally as the Son of David. In fact, His ministry is based on David's kingship, and David was not a perfect man!

Many churches today would ban David from ministering or having any place of authority in the church on the basis of his failures. But Jesus is content to be known as the son of an imperfect man! That really challenged me! If Jesus is able to be a son to an imperfect man, then there must be something wrong with my perspective. I didn't want to be a son to an imperfect person, but Jesus was happy to be known as the son of an imperfect man. I couldn't escape this reality. I was trapped!

I didn't know it then, but that day was going to determine the rest of my life. Finally, I had to be honest and admit, "Lord, I'm *nobody's* son. And what is more, I don't want to be. I'm scared of that. Would You help me?" When I said, "Would You help me?" His presence immediately left the room and I was alone by myself in the chapel. I felt that the Lord had gone to start the work on my problem.

FINDING THE HEART OF SONSHIP

Following this encounter, the Lord began to work on me to restore the heart of a son. The first thing, as I wrote in the previous chapter, was to be able to forgive my Dad from the heart. When I came to this point my heart was free but then I began to wonder how I could get the heart of a son restored to me.

I couldn't come up with any answers for that. I was thinking and praying about it a lot but nothing seemed to come to the fore. How do you get the heart of a son back when you have lost it? Well, when you lose anything, where will you find it? You will find it in the place where you left it! Right? If you can go back to where you lost it, it will be there. It is as simple as that.

So I had lost the heart of a son, in my relationship with my Dad. That was where I had closed it down so, to get the heart of a son back, I thought it would have something to do with my Dad, but I didn't know exactly what. I couldn't think of any way that I could possibly find the heart of a son again. After a while I began to realize that there was one thing I could do. I had forgiven my father for all of the things that he did and didn't do, however I realized that I also had treated him in a way that was not good. I had closed my heart to him. I could have been more gracious and more forgiving. I could have been more grateful and honouring of him. It was my choice to cut him out of my heart. It then occurred to me that I could write a letter to him and ask for his forgiveness for all of those things.

When I was a boy at home, one of my chores was to mow the lawn at the rear of the house. I never once did it without my father putting pressure on me to do it. I never did it willingly and I never did it well. I would try to avoid the corners and ignore areas that needed to be cut. I would also avoid my responsibility by going out after I got home from school and staying out until darkness fell so that there was no time to mow the lawn. I would be glad when it was raining and I used this as an excuse. If it weren't raining I would go down to the creek to swim or catch eels. Finally my father would put pressure on me and make different threats, such as taking away my opportunities to play so I would reluctantly and begrudgingly mow the lawn. I never once did it willingly. I was thinking that I could ask his forgiveness for this and for other things.

There was a real problem with this however. In our house, nobody ever said that they were sorry because that was perceived as weakness. No one ever asked forgiveness and no one ever said, "I love you." Those were signs of weakness and so I was afraid to ask for my father's forgiveness in case he used it as leverage against me in the next argument.

THE LETTER

I decided to draft a letter to see how it might read but I didn't feel that I could take the step of actually sending it. Eventually I expressed in the letter what I wanted to express. I asked his forgiveness for never having mowed the lawn the way that he wanted it mowed. I asked forgiveness for not having the right attitude towards him. I asked forgiveness for the arguments. I asked forgiveness for things that I had said to him. I asked his forgiveness for not doing many of the chores he wanted me to do. At the end of the letter I said, "I ask your forgiveness for closing my heart to you when I was ten years old and for not being a son to you." Then I put the letter on the shelf where it sat for two weeks until I mentioned it to Jack Winter who retorted, "Well, you had better post it!" and walked off!

Now the pressure was on! I bought an envelope and a stamp, put the address on it, put it in the envelope and put it back on the shelf where it sat for a month. I knew when I wrote it that it said what I wanted to say but I didn't want to reread it, because I was chickening out. Finally, I knew I had to send it. I knew that Jack would ask me one day if had I sent the letter and I wanted to say that I had sent it, so I decided that I would take the letter "for a walk." I reassured myself that I would not actually send it. I would just go for a walk by the post box.

Close to where we were staying there was a red letterbox on the side of the road. I walked up to it and put the letter into the slot and thought, "If I drop this he will get it." I quickly pulled it out again and walked on down the road. I went about thirty yards and knew that I had to send it. I came back, put it back in the slot – and dropped it! Immediately I felt like I had been kicked in the stomach. I cried the whole way back to where we were staying, went straight up to our bedroom, lay on the bed and wept. I was afraid of my father's reaction when he received the letter.

After that we went up to northern Minnesota to a campsite that Jack Winter's ministry had bought. We were driving up to this new ministry centre and I said to Denise, "When we get to this place, I would really like to be a son to the leadership there." I had never thought in those terms before and I was surprised that the words came out of my mouth! It was the first sign of change! It was while we were there that Jack Winter came and preached again on the Father's love. I had heard him speak on it many times but never really understood it. I would kneel down beside him while he was praying for people to experience the Father's love. I would see them weeping as the hurts of their life were healed and I was sensing the anointing but not understanding what was going on.

AN IMPARTATION OF THE FATHER'S LOVE

After listening to Jack preaching on the Father's love this time, I said to him, "Jack, I finally understand what you are talking about. Would you pray for me?" He had been looking for an opportunity to pray for me so he agreed. He took me into a little room in the back of the ministry centre and I sat in the only chair in the room. Jack knelt down beside me and looked me right in the eye. "Can you be a little boy who needs to be loved?" he asked.

I thought, "I'm a twenty-nine year-old man. I'm not a little boy!" but when I looked into Jack's eyes, somehow I knew that he was seeing me for who I really was. On the outside I was fit, strong, and capable but on the inside I was a little boy who needed to be loved because I had never known a father's love.

The truth is, if you have never known a father's love, then you still need a father's love today. And so I said to him, "I don't know, Jack, but I can try." He asked me to put my arms around his neck like a little boy who needed to hug his dad. I had never hugged a man in my entire life but I put my arms around his neck. It felt extremely awkward and I wanted to escape from it and run from the room but he quickly put his arms around me and held me very tight. He was giving me a clear message that I was not getting out of this until he was finished! He then prayed a very simple prayer, "Father, would You come now and make my arms to be Your arms around this young man." In that moment I wasn't being held by Jack any more, I was being held by God. He continued, "Would You pour Your love into his heart because he has never known a Father like You." After two or three minutes he was done and I stood up.

From that moment on, it seemed that everything was different. Whenever I would start to pray, the word "Father" came spontaneously from my mouth. I felt as if my spirit had touched the Father. In reality it was the Father who had touched my spirit.

Some months later we flew back to New Zealand. We went to stay with Denise's mother in Taupo, where we live now. We stayed there for two weeks, but I did not want to visit my parents because I was afraid to discover my father's reaction to that letter. After a couple of weeks I finally said to Denise, "We really must go. Let's go and get it over and done with." So we got in the car, made the drive, and spent the afternoon with my parents then drove back to Taupo. My father never mentioned the letter.

We visited them again a few months later but he still didn't mention it. Another visit a few months after that, and he still didn't mention it. Five years went past. Now I was thirty-five years old, my father had never mentioned the letter and I began to wonder if he had even got it. Then one day I asked my mother, "When we were back in the States a few years ago, I wrote a letter to Dad. Do you know if he got the letter or not?" My mother said, "Oh yes! He got it! In fact, he still has it. He keeps it in a drawer beside his bed!" When she said that, I realized that the letter was precious to my Dad. It was too precious to bring up in an argument. My father would never have been able to say, "I forgive you, son." I had never heard him say, "I'm sorry" or, "I love you" or anything like that. He never talked in those ways but I realized that it was precious to him and so I assumed that he had forgiven me. The years went on and I decided one day that I was going to tell my father that I loved him.

I didn't feel any love for my father in my heart, but my thought was that if I said it through willpower, then God would honour that with the feelings of love. In the same way that builders pour concrete into a timber framework that they have laid, my declaration of love would provide the framework for God to pour the stuff in. I would say the words, "I love you" and trust that God might give me the feelings of love for my father. In truth, I would have rather climbed Mount Everest. It was a huge thing to try to do. But in all of the arguments I had with my father, he had taught me one thing and that was to say things that might be hard for the other person to hear. In fact, that was very easy for me to do in those days. So I made the decision to tell him that I loved him.

"I LOVE YOU, DAD!"

The next time we visited them I was looking for an opportunity to say it. I was hoping that he would go into the kitchen and I would follow him, get myself a glass of water and say, "By the way, Dad, I love you," and walk back to the living room, but he didn't go into the kitchen and so I could never get him alone. Finally we were leaving the house to drive home and I was thinking that I had missed my opportunity. My dad had a particular habit. Whenever people would visit he would always stand in the kitchen, which guests had to go through to leave the house. He would stand with his back to the refrigerator and shake hands with people as they went out. My father didn't teach me many things in my life but when I was four years old he taught me how to shake hands. I can still remember it word for word in exact detail. He said, "When you shake hands with a man – firm grip – none of this limp-wristed stuff. Shake two or three times and then let go. You don't touch a man for too long!"

So we were leaving the house and I shook my dad's hand – two or three shakes, firm grip, let go – and I walked out the door. He shook hands with the others and we left the house. As I came to the corner of the house outside I thought, "I'll do it now!" so as I looked back past my family to Mum and Dad and said, "Goodbye Mum and Dad. I love you, Dad!" and walked round the corner quickly. Denise and the kids followed quickly on my heels to the car and we drove away! I didn't hear a scream or a crash so I got away with it!

The *next* time we were visiting them I thought that I would do the same thing again. I would say, "I love you" again. This time as I shook his hand at the refrigerator, I did as before – firm grip, two or three shakes – but this time I didn't let go and he looked up at me. I looked him straight in the eye and said, "I love you, Dad" and I let him go and walked out of the house. When I got out onto the lawn, I looked back into the house and saw my dad still standing there, looking at his hand. My father had never heard those words spoken to him in all of his life, particularly by a man. My mother had said them for a time before and when they were first married but then stopped. With my courage growing I decided that I would do the same thing again the next visit.

As we were leaving he put out his hand to shake my hand and I thought it was a bit tentative! This time, however, instead of taking his hand, I put my arm inside his arm, and hugged him for the first time in my life and whispered, "I love you, Dad" into his ear. He gave an almost imperceptible nod of the head but it was like hugging a tree. Every muscle in his body was rigid. After that, I would take the opportunity to say, "I love you, Dad" each time we visited.

It was three years later when my father called me on the phone one night. My mother always made the telephone calls, and this was the second time in my entire life that my father phoned me. He said, "There's a rugby game in the city near you and I'm coming to see the game. I wonder if I could come and stay with you overnight?" Then he added, "There's something I want to say to you." My father had never stayed in our home before. He had only ever visited our home once or twice and we had been married eighteen years by now. He came after the game and Denise made a nice dinner. We ate the dinner and then he said, "There's something I want to say to you," so Denise got busy at the other end of the house and left us alone together.

We sat there all evening and he couldn't say it. He would bring the subject back again and again. He would say, "I've come because I want to say something to you. I want to say this to you." In the midst of that he would look at me, as if he was desperate to get the words out but he couldn't and so he would just start talking about the rugby again, or something else. It was at that time that he said to me, "I've never heard these words spoken to me in all of my life except by your mother." He also said, "As far as I understand, men don't say these words to each other." And he said another time, "During the war, you don't make friends with anybody, because when they die, you can't do your job." All these things came out as he was sitting with me.

Now I am the youngest in my family. My brother is a scientist and my parents proudly attended all his graduation ceremonies. He was the first person in our family that ever went to university, probably all the way back to Adam in the garden! My sister worked in television and my parents would watch the credits at the end of the television program each Thursday night just to see her name. They were very proud of her. I had the greatest academic potential in our family but all I wanted was to become a deer culler and a recluse and live in the hills. I didn't do anything that my parents wanted me to do and my father was not proud of me. He felt that I had let him down. When I became a Christian it was even worse. It became something else to argue about. During that night, however, when he stayed with us after the rugby game, he said, "There's something else I need to say to you."

He became very serious. It was very difficult to talk about these things but he said to me, "There may come a time when only your mother or I are left alive," and that was all he said. He looked at me as if to say, "Please understand what I am saying. Please don't make me say it all!" I was shocked that he was asking me. I was his youngest son, and the one that had failed to fulfill his expectations. All I could say to him was, "Dad, if there is ever a time when you are left alone, you can come and live with us." His shoulders visibly relaxed as if a weight had been lifted from his mind but he still hadn't said what he had come for.

The hours wore on and finally it was almost midnight and he brought the subject up again. He said, "I've come because I want to say this to you." He got close but he couldn't say it. Finally he said, "I want you to know," as he looked at me with pleading eyes, "Help me to say this!" There was nothing I could do to help him. All I could do was sit and wait and finally.... He never said it but he got close. He forced out the words, "I want you to know that your mother and I love all you kids." I replied, "I love you too, Dad" and he nodded his head as if to acknowledge what he really meant to say.

"I LOVE YOU, SON!"

The years passed and my father eventually said to me one day the words, "I love you son!" It was in 2001 and he had been hospitalized for six or seven years. Diabetes had cost him his right leg and his eyesight was greatly diminished. He couldn't watch television. All he could see was the brightness of the window and there was nothing of interest outside the window. He had suffered a number of minor strokes and lost his short-term memory although his long-term memory was still intact. I went to see him because we were going away on a long ministry trip to Europe and, for the first time in my life, I was able to have a conversation with him in which he was not argumentative. All of the arguments had gone out of him.

I told him how I had felt when I was a boy during all the arguments that we used to have. He was just listening and understanding, with no argument left in him. As we were talking he said three times, "I'm so sorry!" My father had never apologized to anyone. Three times that day he said, "I love you, son!" As I was going out the door he said, "Oh, by the way!" I turned round and he said, "You know, I always loved you!"

I remember going round to my mum's place having left him in the hospital and telling her what we had talked about and what Dad had said, and she said, "When you used to slam the door and walk out into the night. Do you know what your father used to do? He would go into the bedroom and lock the door. He wouldn't allow me in there, because he was crying."

Sometime later we were in England and we were finishing what had been an exhausting schedule of meetings. It was the final meeting and we were praying for the last few people. One of the men in the church came up to me and said, "James, there's a telephone call for you from New Zealand. It's your brother." I knew what it was, of course. I had wondered what I would do if my father passed away when I was overseas. Should I cancel conferences? Should I go back? Does it really matter? What should I do?

So I went and talked to my brother and he told me that Dad had passed away half an hour previously and that he insisted that I come home and take his funeral. I flew back to New Zealand while Denise stayed in England. The funeral took place the day after I arrived back and I expressed my surprise that Dad would want me to take the funeral. He had always argued with me and gave me the impression that he was strongly opposed to Christianity.

I remember standing at the front as I spoke at the funeral. There was quite a crowd there and as I looked around the room I wondered if there was anyone there who genuinely loved my father. He had argued with everybody. As I looked at the casket beside me I thought, "Maybe he wanted me to take the funeral because he knew that I had the heart of a son for him and that I am a real son to him."

THE HEART OF SONSHIP

That was my life with my father. As I look back, the most wonderful part about it for me was the moment when I put the envelope in the slot. Why? Because, when I dropped that envelope containing the letter, God restored to me the heart of a son and that was the doorway for me to come to know my heavenly Father.

I believe that most of us have lost the heart of a son towards our natural father or mother. How do we get it back? We will find it again in the place that we have lost it.

The truth is, you cannot really know the Father unless you have the heart of a son or daughter. You can receive a touch from Him. You can have an experience of His love. You can even know His love touching your heart and your emotions. But you cannot have an intimate relationship with Him as Father unless you have the heart of a son. Many people encounter the heavenly Father but only those who have the heart of a son or the heart of a daughter can live in relationship with Him as a father. As you come to know Him as a father and His love begins to touch and fill your heart, that selfsame love, over time, will continuously heal your heart. That love available, will continue to pour into the ground of your being until it fills all of the holes and when it has filled all of the holes it begins to rise in its level and bring you to a place where His love will be like a mighty ocean that you swim in.

Because so many of us have closed our hearts to our earthly fathers and have lost the hearts of sons and daughters, perhaps you too have a letter to write to one or both of your parents. Perhaps a phone call, or a face-to-face talk would be more appropriate. I leave it to you to decide, but there are two things I know for sure. Firstly: if you don't have the heart of a son to the parents that God gave to you, you cannot have a real relationship with God as your Father, and you will go through your life trapped in your orphan ways and perspectives.

The second thing is this: if you are in some form of Christian ministry you will continually face a barrier to your effectiveness because to be like Jesus you first have to be a son at heart. If you don't have the heart of a son your capacity to speak and act like Jesus from your heart is limited. Hebrews 1:1 says, "In the past God spoke through prophets but today He has spoken through His Son." He still prefers to speak through sons! This revealing of the Father and His love is crucial for the future of the Church, as well as for our own individual lives.

Now that is a very interesting statement. *"From one man He made every nation of men, that they should inhabit the whole earth."* Inhabiting the earth was actually a commission from the Garden of Eden. Humanity was supposed to spread out and inhabit the whole earth. Then the apostle continued,

"...and He determined the times set for them and the exact places where they should live."

Let me make a brief comment here: it isn't the main point that I want to make, but this is an interesting statement that Paul makes here. God predetermined the time of our birth and the place of our birth. We come from different nations and cultures. Those who founded or populated the nations weren't necessarily trying to do the will of God, but in the midst of it all, somehow the time and place of your birth was part of His plan for all of mankind. It is no mistake that I'm a New Zealander and that you are the nationality that you are. It's no mistake because it was *God* who determined the times set for you and the exact places where you should live. He did this so that humanity would seek Him.

Then Paul makes another very interesting statement in which he quotes a secular Greek poet. You need to understand that Paul was intellectually brilliant. As a student he sat at the feet of Gamaliel who was the leading teacher of his particular sect of the Pharisees. He was at the very top level of the students of his day. He said that he surpassed the others that were in his class. (Galatians1: 14) In another place (2 Corinthians 11:5) he states that he was "not inferior" to anyone. He grew up in a town called Tarsus, which was a university city of the Roman Empire. It is without doubt that he had reached the zenith of religious observation and knowledge.

By the time he was twelve years old he would have already memorized vast portions of the books of Genesis, Exodus, Leviticus, Numbers and Deuteronomy. That was the normal expectation of a boy in his particular place. He was a bright young boy, and I imagine (because he was brought up in a university city) that he and his family would have had exposure to the many cultures of the Roman Empire. Doubtless he would have been very exposed to Greek culture, which would have been the dominant culture of the time and he had most likely learned a Greek poem (of Aratus, a poet who had lived in his home town of Tarsus), which he was able to recall. In this passage, Paul was speaking to a group of Greeks who were the leading philosophers of the city in Athens. We know that these Greeks were anxious to avoid offending any of the gods. They were very religious in their philosophy and wanted to cover all their bases, so to speak. So they built an altar to honour "the unknown god."

These philosophers heard that Paul was preaching in the city so they asked him to come and speak to them. While he was speaking to them he quoted this particular Greek poet. It amuses me that a Greek poet has at least one line of his poem that has ended up being recorded in Holy Scripture. I am sure that he didn't realize he was writing Scripture when he penned his verse. What is more, Paul quoted it as truth, that it was actually the wisdom of God. It is inspired Scripture and as such it is breathed by the Spirit of God. Somewhere along the way God breathed upon what this Greek poet had written, and Paul used it to win over these Greek philosophers. He said,

"In Him (meaning the Jewish God) *we live and move and have our being. As some of your own poets have said, 'For we indeed are His offspring.'"*

In verse 29 he continued, *"Therefore, since we are God's offspring..."*

Now, I had read this passage many times before I really noticed it. When I noticed this, it came as something of a quandary to me because Paul was speaking to a *totally non-Christian* audience and said to them, "We are God's offspring. We are God's children." You see, I had been taught that I became God's son when I *became a Christian*. I became His child the moment I was born again, and unless I am born again I cannot enter the kingdom of God. And that is absolutely true. However, there seemed to be a problem here as I was reading this because Paul was saying to these Greek philosophers, "Therefore since we are God's children, since we are His offspring, since we came from Him, since we are His children...." My problem was that I couldn't understand how Paul could possibly say that these non-Christian Greeks were God's children!

I want to state very clearly at this point, that we will never experience any of the benefits of being children of God unless we are born again. That is absolute and there is no argument about it. But there has to be something more in what Paul was saying here for this to be inspired Scripture and to actually be true. I was always told that before I was a Christian, I walked in darkness. I was told, in fact, that Satan himself was my father because I was walking in his ways. But Paul stated here that we *all, even* those who are not "born again" are the offspring of God. This took me by surprise, because I had always been taught that we were born of the Spirit of God, and that being born of God's Spirit is our entrance into being God's children. Paul was saying something else, however, which sounded like something that we would not consider to be conventional Christian doctrine. It actually sounds like a form of Universalism. So I was trying to understand this and the Lord began to give me some insight.

As we consider this, it is crucial to understand something: When God first created Adam and Eve in the Garden of Eden, His purpose for them was that they *would not* sin. Theologians have argued for centuries on this issue of whether God knew beforehand that Adam and Eve would end up sinning. There is no consensus on this at all. However, what we do know is that God's plan for Adam and Eve was a *real* plan. His purpose was that they *would not* sin, so for us to understand this issue of every person in the world being God's child, we need to understand the meaning of the word *redemption*.

REDEMPTION

What redemption really means is "to buy back."

I am wearing a watch that I received as a Christmas gift. It was bought for me, so I could never say that this watch has been redeemed. It was bought, but it wasn't redeemed. When Jesus bought us with a price He purchased us *back*, He *redeemed* us. Buying my watch could never be described as "redeeming" for one simple reason. You can only redeem something that you have previously owned. The redemption that Jesus accomplished through His death on the cross was therefore a buying back of what God had previously owned. Jesus didn't buy us. He bought us back!

Therefore, in a real sense, Christianity is truly described in terms of redemption when we understand that *before* we were sinners we *actually belonged* to God. That belonging did not originate in our lifetime, but it began in the life of our forefathers, Adam and

Eve. When they were on this earth each and every one of us was in them because we all came from out of them. The whole human race was contained within Adam and Eve and belonged to God, prior to the fall. What was God's purpose for us? His purpose was that Adam and Eve would never sin and continue to multiply as He commanded. They would multiply and fill the earth and subdue it. This was God's commission for them to accomplish. His purpose (and it was a real plan) was that mankind would fill the earth without Adam and Eve or anyone else ever sinning.

THE ORIGINAL PLAN

Imagine what the world would have been like if Adam and Eve had never sinned. Can you imagine what your life would be like? It would be very different from how you have experienced it. If Adam and Eve had never sinned, they would still be alive today! You could go to their house and knock on the door, and Adam would come to the door and invite you in. They would have been alive now for a very long time, but they would still be in their prime. I believe that if Adam walked into a room today, everyone present would immediately fall down and worship him because of his appearance. We would think that he was God, because Adam was made in the image of God.

If sin and death had not entered, Adam and Eve would have looked right into the very face of God Himself every day for thousands of years. It would not be a limited revelation, but they would gaze on the total revelation of all that God is. When Moses went up the mountain and came back down, his face was so filled with the glory of God that great fear came upon the people. He had to cover himself with a veil so that they would be able to handle the way he looked after just forty days on the mountain. Adam and Eve would have walked with God for *thousands* of years. What is more, every person who had ever been born would still be alive today - which means your parents, grandparents, great-grandparents, and beyond! Every single human being would be alive because there would have been no such thing as death.

Death is a very difficult thing for us to deal with because there is nothing in us that was created to deal with it. Any form of rejection, loneliness or trauma is difficult to deal with because we do not have an inbuilt resource to handle them. We were not designed for this world as it stands today. We were designed for a world in which Adam and Eve had never sinned.

Consider another major difference. Every single person who ever came into contact with you throughout your entire life would have *only* expressed absolute love, acceptance, and wonder towards you. They would be filled with the sense of how amazingly beautiful you are, and how exciting you are to be with. They would celebrate the incredible gifting and resources that have entered the earth because you are here. The sense of welcome for each one of us as we were born into this world would be so life affirming, it would have a tremendous effect upon us.

We cannot possibly imagine the sense of joy that we would have experienced had Adam and Eve never sinned. It is hard to fathom but *this is* the life that God designed for us to live. Imagine what it was like for Adam to be formed as an adult human being with a full resource of mind, emotion, heart and will, as well as the full ability to understand and think properly. His intellect would have been far beyond that of any of us. According to scientists, we only use ten percent of our brain's capacity. Adam would have been fully operational with one hundred percent of his mental and intellectual capacity. He came into this world and immediately received and experienced the totality of the love of God poured into his being without hindrance.

The very entrance of his life into this world would have been saturated with a sense of how wonderful and loved he was, because he would have looked right into the eyes of God the Father as soon as he became conscious. As Adam opened his eyes, which are the windows of the soul, and gazed into the face of God the Father, his soul would have been infused with the person of the Father. You see, God *is* love, and His purpose was that every son and daughter of Adam and Eve would be filled with that same love, that same revelation, that same substance, every single day of their lives throughout history and eternity.

We were designed for this kind of existence. *We were designed so that our natural birth would be our entrance into the complete experience of God being our Father.* Our natural birth would usher us into the blessing of knowing God as our Father and us being His sons and daughters. We would never have a word for "security" because we would never have a conscious ability to conceive of anything less than total peace and security. The concept of fear would not exist.

Your mother and father would not be the people that you have experienced them to be. They would have parented you very differently. Their parents (your grandparents) would have been so saturated with the love of God the Father themselves, that their love for your parents would have been a perfect expression of God Himself, far beyond anything that you have ever experienced. Let me repeat it one more time. *Our natural birth would have been our entrance into all of the blessing of God being our Father,* and of knowing His presence, His provision, His love, His care and His direction into every single blessing in His heart for us.

SECOND BIRTH

However, as we know only too well, Adam and Eve *did* sin. And because Adam and Eve sinned, God had to design a *second birth* to bring us all into the knowledge of His love as our Father, and to bring us into all of the experience of Him being a father to us. So, when He sent Jesus to die for us, the Father was opening a door and Jesus became that door. Jesus didn't open the door. He *is* the door.

God the Father opened the door for us to come back to Him. To be *bought back* so that we could once again have access to everything that Adam and Eve lost. *That is what it means to be redeemed!* The whole purpose of God sending His Son to the earth for us was to *redeem* everything that had been lost when Adam and Eve sinned. In fact, He has redeemed *more* than what was lost. Because, instead of being sons and daughters of God like Adam was we have (in Christ) become a part of the life of God Himself. What a wonderful thing! When we are born again it is so that we would come to know Him as our Father in the same way that Adam and Eve would have known Him if the fall had never occurred. When we see this it gives us a glimpse of what it truly means to be a Christian. It gives us an insight into our destiny and the work of God in our life.

This full understanding of redemption is crucial to ministering effectively in the lives of others. God's ultimate purpose is to restore your life and my life to what *it would have been had Adam and Eve never sinned*. That is the purpose of the cross and the purpose of redemption. It is the purpose of becoming a Christian. The purpose of *everything* that God is doing in our life is to restore us to the original sinless state of Adam and Eve. It is very worthwhile for us to meditate upon what life would be like for us and how we would feel about ourselves if we had been born into that world. God wants us to know His love for us because love puts a foundation deep inside us that gives us absolute security of soul.

When you know that God loves you, there is no struggle with the doctrine of God being your provider. Often you can strive to believe that He will provide for your material needs. You can stand on the promises of God, you can exercise faith and you can believe God as hard as you wish. You can make positive confessions and repeat personal affirmations to get this truth into you. However, if you don't really know in your heart that God the Father loves you, you will have great difficulty being able to hold on to the fact that He is going to look after you. But when you have a foundation deep inside you that God is your Father and that He loves you, then you are not going to have any difficulty believing that He is going to look after you in this life. Love is the foundation of faith; in fact, love is the foundation of *everything* in our Christian life. Experiencing and walking in the love of God the Father is what it is all about.

Many people are portraying that the way to godliness is to appropriate this by constantly reciting truth statements to yourself. You will never be convinced that way. But when His love fills your spirit and you *know* that He loves you, the Bible becomes a different book. We have been chosen before the foundation of the world. We didn't choose Him, rather He chose us for an incredible life that is eternal and has started now! *This is* eternity for us, right now! The purpose, the plan, the direction that God has for our life is to redeem us, so that our life will be everything that He planned for it to be, *before* the fall. "Paradise lost" has been regained in Christ!

HE CONCEIVED YOU

The prophet Jeremiah writes,

"The word of the Lord came to me saying 'Before I formed you in the womb I knew you, before you were born I set you apart, I appointed you as a prophet to the nations." (Jeremiah 1:4)

We cannot assume from this that we are all appointed as prophets to the nations. In a general sense that is true and it may be specifically true for some, as it was for Jeremiah. I believe, however, that the first part of the verse is relevant to every one of us because it is speaking about the creation of Jeremiah. *"Before I formed you in the womb I knew you."* I really had trouble understanding this. What *did* the Lord mean? *How* could He know Jeremiah before he was in his mother's womb? If you look at it from a purely biological viewpoint, Jeremiah didn't actually exist before being in his mother's womb. This is not talking about reincarnation, either. Reincarnation is not part of the biblical understanding of human life. So, how could the Lord know Jeremiah before he was in his mother's womb? Make no mistake about it. He *really did* know Jeremiah.

There is only one way that this statement could possibly be true. Far back in time, before Jeremiah was in his mother's womb, God conceived in His mind the very person that Jeremiah would become. He designed Jeremiah's entire person, his physical being, his mental capacity, his emotional and spiritual makeup, the gifts and talents that he would have. God could say, long before Jeremiah was in his mother's womb, "I know exactly who this person is going to be."

Dear reader, I believe that it is the same for each and every one of us. Far back in time God conceived *you* in His heart and mind.

He made you the unique person that you are with the specific natural abilities that you have. Your mother and father most likely didn't know whether you would be a boy or a girl but *He* knew you right down to the finest detail. He knew how tall you would be, how heavy you would be (give or take a few pounds), He knew what colour your hair would be. He knew your personality and what talents you would have. He gave each of us certain abilities that others don't have. He limited us in certain other abilities. He designed *exactly* the person that you would be. He knew you. You need to understand that He is your *real* Father, because *He* conceived you in his mind and heart before your natural conception.

What is even more amazing is that He conceived every one of us in love because He *is* love. In other words, when He decided that He was going to make you, in His mind He thought, "How can I make this one absolutely lovable?" *He designed every one of us in absolute love.* Some people feel that they are a mistake, and that they shouldn't be here on this earth. This is very personal to me. My mother said to me, "When your dad and I got married we really wanted to have a little boy first. So, when your brother came along we were really pleased. Then we thought it would be wonderful to have a little girl and your sister came along. We were so pleased and we decided that we wouldn't have any more children." She continued, "Then we discovered that you were coming." Then she paused and said, "But when *you* came you brought your own love with you." In other words, "For nine months we really didn't want you!"

Many people have had a similar experience and they constantly feel like they shouldn't actually be on this earth. It may be that their parents *had* to get married because of the pregnancy and consequently they felt as if they have been a problem ever since.

The wonderful reality is this: God our Father conceived everyone of us in His love before we were even in our mother's womb. You are a love conception by your REAL FATHER!

There is no such thing as illegitimate children. There are only illegitimate parents, because every child who has ever come to this world is loved and wanted by God our Father. That is why He was able to say by the Spirit through Paul in the book of Acts, that we *all* (Christian or not) are His offspring. He was able to say this because in His original plan for mankind He designed each one of us.

I have often wondered, "At what point did He actually design me? Was it just five minutes before I was conceived?" Was He taken by surprise saying, "Oh no! Here comes another one! Quick! Make another one!" How long ago did He actually design me? Was it just minutes before my birth? Was it years? I believe, in fact, that He designed every one of us before He even made a single atom of this universe, because He was not *after a universe, He was after a family.* His purpose was not that He would have this wonderful creation. Rather, He made this creation as an environment for us to live in. We look up at the stars and imagine them going on forever. Do you know why He made it like that? Not so that we would be overwhelmed or despair about our existence, but so that we can look at it and go "wow!" So that everything in us would be filled with wonder about Him. He made the universe to give us an impression of the type of Father we really have. Isn't He great!!

MADE IN HIS IMAGE

Many people go through this life feeling like they don't belong anywhere or that they shouldn't have been born. Some people feel so much like trespassers in their life that they don't feel that they even belong in their own home. They spend their entire life working and saving to pay off a mortgage so that they can own a home and finally they get their certificate of ownership but they still live as if they shouldn't be in this world. The plain and simple fact is that we are our heavenly Father's kids.

Far back in time He decided that He was going to have you, and *the day that you came into this world was a day that He had been looking forward to for thousands of years.* The only thing that tainted it for Him was knowing that, because of the Fall, your natural birth would not bring you into all the blessing of His being your Father. He still loves us as a Father but unless we are born again we will never experience any of the benefits of His actually *being* a Father to us. He sent Jesus to die for us so that we could be born again and our *second birth* would bring us into all the blessing of having God as our Father.

Let's also look at Psalm 139:16. The NIV puts it like this,

"Your eyes saw my unformed body"

Way back in time, before your body was formed in your mother's womb, God saw it. He knew what your physical body would look like before the world was made. You are not a result of evolutionary processes and therefore a freak of nature with no purpose or reason to exist. Your parents didn't know if you would be a boy or a girl or at least had no say over which you would be. But way back, when God determined the times set for you and the exact places where you would live, *He* knew what you would look like.

I know that some people are born with physical malformations of blindness, deafness and worse. Somehow, humanity's opening the doors of sin and its vulnerability to Satan's destructiveness has allowed these things to happen. Some of the reason is down to human error in medicine, and perhaps we will find out more in the future about things that we humans do that cause other things to happen too.

The truth is, however, that before you were in your mother's womb, God knew what your physical body would look like and *He* says that we are fearfully and wonderfully made.

Our daughter was an international model for ten years. I always thought she was beautiful, even when she first got up in the morning. I remember asking her once, "These supermodels, do they think they are beautiful?" and she replied, "Not one of them." Every single one would say that there was a part of themselves that they were not happy with. Their knees were too knobbly, their nose was too big or their eyes were too small. This only goes to demonstrate the innate sense that something of God's incredible creation in us has been stolen away.

He who is beauty itself can make nothing ugly. The heart of an artist is expressed through his paintings and there is none more beautiful than God Himself. Therefore, when He made you and I, it was an expression of His own nature. He made us beautiful. Many people go through their whole life never feeling like they are good enough for public scrutiny, never really able to stand in front of others. They feel a deep sense of shame about themselves. They feel shy. They cover themselves with veils of separation because they don't feel acceptable in their looks, interests or lifestyle. God made every one of us and He conceived every aspect of our being.

Many people feel that God made the man in His image and that the woman was just thrown in to help, so to speak. She was created to slave, to work alongside the man. What they don't realize, however, is that the woman was *also* made in the image of God. They don't realize that femininity and womanhood (as well as masculinity) is an expression of the nature of God Himself. The feminine is also an expression of what God is like. I know a woman who doesn't have any mirrors in her house because she is convinced that she is ugly and the mirror only seems to confirm that perception. The fact is that God never made anything ugly, and if people can't see how beautiful you are it only shows the difference between them and God, because He thinks that I am beautiful and He thinks that you are too!

Somehow this whole Hollywood and celebrity culture has presented an ideal of beauty and a perception of 'good looks' that nobody can possibly fulfill. It robs a sense of confidence about our appearance. The saying goes, "If the barn needs painting then we'll paint it." I'm not against putting on makeup. When I have been interviewed for television they told me that I had to wear makeup. The first time it happened I couldn't believe it! It took a lot of washing to get it off! The simple fact is this; God made you beautiful and if people can't see it, it's not your problem; it's their problem.

God Himself is the One who knows me best and He is the One who loves me most. He knows all of my faults and He still loves me absolutely. We cannot say, "I don't love this person because they have got so many faults." When we are unable to love somebody or unable to express love to others, it only highlights the difference between us and God. God our Father conceived each one of us in His mind and in His love, and He created us to be completely lovable. *He is our real Father.* He is and always *has been* your *real* Father.

You have only been on loan to your parents. They didn't know anything about you but He did. He conceived the very unique features of each individual human being. He designed everything about us. He is our real Father and, if we receive Christ and walk in His life, we will know our heavenly Father for the rest of eternity.

RESTORED TO BE SONS AND DAUGHTERS

When we are talking about God being our Father, or about receiving the Father's love, we are not just talking about God coming into our life and giving us an experience or a touch of His love to heal our emotional hurts. Those things do take place, but what it is ultimately about is that God is restoring us to be His sons and daughters. He is redeeming us to come to know Him as our Father just as Adam knew Him, and more than that, like Jesus knew Him.

It is God the Father's intent that we would come to walk with Him in eternity as sons appropriate to who He is. That is where He is taking us. To me, this is the most exciting issue of realizing that God is my Father. To know that everything that I am was designed by my heavenly Father and that I am His son. From eternity to eternity, I am His son. Of course I'm not Jesus, but the glorious truth is that "in Christ" He has become *my* Father and I am His son now and forever. He has always purposed it to be that way. He had to redeem me because of what happened in the garden, but I was always His son, and I always will be.

The Father has been waiting for thousands of years, for the moment when you came into the world. When you came, He celebrated because He knew you long before you were in your mother's womb. He has been waiting for the day when your spirit finally receives the revelation that He is your *real* Father. Like every loving parent who looks forward to the day when their child says, "Daddy!" for the first time, God the Father has been waiting thousands of years for you to look up and see Him, and cry out from the depths of your heart, "Papa!"

CHAPTER 6

The Orphan Spirit

~

I first heard the term "orphan spirit" at a conference in Toronto in 2002. I heard the Lord say it fifteen minutes before I was due to speak. I quickly opened my Bible and a verse that I had read many times before struck me and everything changed. I went up to the podium and the whole message came together as I spoke. I didn't know what my message was going to be, but this verse was suddenly enlightened to me and has become one of our most well known messages in this whole revelation of the Father. You could say, in fact, that it has become the flagship teaching of our ministry, providing the foundational paradigm that we teach from.

The verse that struck me is from John 14, which Jesus spoke in His last days, approximately a week before He was crucified. Jack Winter once said that a man's last words are likely to be among the most important words he will ever say. When I read this particular verse in Toronto that day I felt like gravity shifted and the earth moved. My Christian life has never been the same since. I have received a number of revelations – but this one has most significantly changed the perspective of how I live my own life. Coming from a Pentecostal/Charismatic theology, it suddenly brought me into a perspective of the Father that I had never seen before.

AN ODD LITTLE VERSE

Before I tell you what the verse is I want to give you some background. The Gospel of John was the first book of the Bible that I ever read. So I had read this verse many times previously yet I hadn't seen its significance. Actually, I thought it was an odd little verse, a verse that I didn't really understand. It contained a word that is not used anywhere else in the book and is used in only one other place in the entire New Testament. In that meeting in Toronto, however, it suddenly jumped off the page at me and changed everything. God opened my understanding to something that I had not seen before.

Let me give you some idea why it impacted me so much. When I was in Bible School, we were given the key words for each chapter of the book of John. By memorizing one word, you could remember what the whole chapter was about. There was a particular verse that was the key to understanding the whole book of John. That verse (John 20:31) says, *"These things are written that you may believe that Jesus is the Son of God, and that by believing, you may have life in His name."* That seemed to make perfect sense to me but when the Lord opened my eyes to this verse in John 14, I saw that this verse could be the key verse to *the whole New Testament, perhaps even the entire Bible.* It is amazing when an "odd little verse" suddenly comes into incredible significance.

The verse that has changed everything for me is John 14:18. It is a simple little verse but there is so much in it. Jesus said it and John wrote it down,

"I will not leave you as orphans. I will come to you."

When this perspective dawned on me I felt, for the first time in my life, that I began to understand the basic problem of humanity. The basic problem not only of our individual struggles, but also the struggles that we have in relationship with each other. The basic problem of church life, the friction between denominations, family disputes and even the wars between nations. I suddenly saw the root problem of humanity's struggle on this earth throughout history. It was a complete paradigm shift.

Someone said to me once, "James, you seem to think that the Father's love is the answer to every problem in humanity." I believe that with all of my heart, because every problem has its foundation in the fact that Adam and Eve lost their place in Eden, lost their place in the Father experientially loving them! When that happened the human race fell from God's total provision and lost intimate fellowship with Him.

So when Jesus said the words, *"I will not leave you as orphans, I will come to you,"* what exactly was He talking about?

WE ARE ALL ORPHANS

I should say firstly that these words did not originate in the heart or mind of Jesus. He said them but they didn't come from *His* thinking or theology. They came from His Father. Jesus said, *"The words that I speak are not My words but I only say what My*

Father has told Me to say. I not only say what My Father has told Me to say but I say it the way He has told Me to say it." (John 12:49 & 50). These words came from the heart of the Father.

When Jesus said the words, "I will not leave you as orphans," you need to realize that He was not speaking these words in an orphanage! The majority of people listening would not have been orphans in the natural sense. We know for a fact that Peter and Andrew were there. They had been fishing with their father when Jesus called them, so we know that they had a father. James and John also had a father. They were the sons of Zebedee (known as the Sons of Thunder). We know that their mother was alive because she came to Jesus and asked that her sons could sit on His right and left in the coming kingdom. She was a follower of Jesus, she believed that He was the Messiah, and she obviously loved her sons and wanted the best for them. So it is clear that they were not orphans.

Only a small percentage of the hearers that day would have actually been orphans, yet the Father's words to them all were, "I will not leave you as orphans. I will come to you." This is God's word to us down through the ages that has been recorded for all time.

Our conclusion is, therefore, that *the Father sees the whole human race as orphans. He sees all of us as orphans.*

THE ORIGINAL ORPHAN SPIRIT

Why does God view the whole human race as orphans? To understand this worldview, that the whole world is in a state of "orphan-ness", we need to go back to its origin. Let us look at Isaiah, chapter 14, which pulls aside the curtain (so to speak) and gives us a glimpse into something that happened before mankind was even created. This is a prophecy that was given by the prophet Isaiah to the king of Babylon and was a contemporary word for its own time. However, many prophecies have more than one application and can often be interpreted on a multiplicity of levels.

From verse 12 onwards it is clear that there is another application that goes much farther back than the time of Isaiah and the king of Babylon. In fact, some versions of the Bible precede this section with a heading called *The Fall of Lucifer*. Many scholars believe that this passage is about the origins of Satan.

The section begins, *"How you are fallen from heaven, O Lucifer, son of the morning? How you are cut down to the ground, you who weakened the nations? For you have said in your heart..."* Then follow five statements that begin with the words, "I will." So we see that the fall of Lucifer began when he decided in his heart, "I will do these things."

"I will ascend into heaven, I will exalt my throne above the stars of God; I will also sit on the mount of the congregation on the farthest sides of the north..." (Isaiah 14:13).

I am not entirely sure of the meaning of this, but I *do* understand the statement *"I will."* He said, *"I will ascend above the heights of the clouds,"* and his final ambition was, *"I will make myself like the Most High."* The ambition that rose in Lucifer's heart was to replace Almighty God, to take His place, and to ultimately become like Him. He was not saying, "I am going to stand alongside God," but rather, *"I will make myself like Him!"* Satan's ambition was not to become like God, but to *replace* Him! If this happened Satan himself would be the ultimate authority in the entire universe.

I believe that this ambition continued to grow in Lucifer to the point where he truly believed that he had succeeded when the Prince of Life was crucified. He didn't understand that there was (in the words of C. S. Lewis) a "deeper magic" in operation that would result in his downfall and ultimate defeat.

The big point that I wish to make here, upon which this whole thing rests is this: When Lucifer formed his dark ambition to replace the Most High, what he was really saying was this: "I will have no father over me!" God is 'father' by His very nature and heaven was always filled with His fatherhood. Therefore, Lucifer was effectively saying, "I do not want a father over me, *I* want to be the father. No one is going to be over me. I am not a son. I am not subject to anybody."

There is a very similar passage in Ezekiel 28:12-19. This time it is Ezekiel who was prophesying to the king of Tyre, and once again there is another layer of meaning, which goes further than the context of the time when it was given. We can get an insight here into the origin of all orphan-ness. Speaking again about Lucifer, it says,

"You were the seal of perfection, full of wisdom and perfect in beauty. You were in Eden, the garden of God; every precious stone was your covering."

As we read this we see that Satan was not created a vile creature. He was known as the "Shining One." He was full of wisdom and perfect in beauty; *"You were in Eden, the garden of God. Every precious stone was your covering."* He was adorned with incredible beauty, the most beautiful of all the beings. He was also filled with wisdom but, because of his own love of his beauty, his wisdom was corrupted. In his original state he had a place in close proximity to the throne of God.

"You were the anointed cherub who covers; I established you; you were on the holy mountain of God. You were perfect in your ways from the day you were created, until iniquity was found in you." (Ezekiel 28:14-15).

This iniquity was the heart ambition to replace God and to get rid of God. It was the ambition to displace God's place in his life so that he could do what he wanted to do and be the ultimate authority in his own life. That is still the basis of all sin today.

Verse 16 says, *"By the abundance of your trading you became filled with violence within, and you sinned,"* and then come these words, *"Therefore I cast you as a profane thing out of the mountain of God."* Verse 17 says, *"Your heart was lifted up because of your beauty,"* Note that it doesn't say that his beauty was actually removed. *"You corrupted your wisdom for the sake of your splendor. I cast you to the ground."*

Other versions use the term, "I expelled you" or, "I threw you to the earth." Jesus Himself saw Satan fall like lightning from heaven. It must have been pretty dramatic! He was cast to the ground, out of God's presence, thrown out of the mountain of God, out of heaven and down to earth, and he took his angels with him.

CAST OUT OF FATHER'S LOVE

I don't know what heaven is like. I haven't been there. All I know is what the Scriptures tell me, that in heaven there is no need for the sun or the moon because God Himself is the light. God fills the heavens. And because God is love, this means that heaven is filled with love.

Imagine what that will be like. We are going to live in an environment where every breath we take will be like breathing liquid love. We will live continually in an environment of total love. There will be no possibility of rejection because total acceptance will be breathed in every second. Absolute and all-pervading love.

Not only is heaven filled with love, it is filled with a specific and particular love. It is filled with a father's love because God is Father. From Him, everything that exists has been birthed. We cannot initiate a single thing. He initiated our salvation and we just responded to the invitation. He initiated creation and we come into everything that He has given to us. By His very essence and nature, God *is* father. It is not something that He became. First and foremost, above all else, and in the deepest sense, His love is a fathering love.

Satan, having rejected God as father, was cast out of heaven, and thrown out of all fathering. He *wanted* to be fatherless. The very essence of his being is that he is *fatherless*. He is an orphan and *wants to be an orphan*. That is why there is no redemption for him. He had the perfect revelation of who God is and chose to reject Him. And thrown to the earth he became the ultimate *orphan spirit*.

The apostle Paul had an insight into what I am saying. In Ephesians 2:2 he wrote, *"You were not only walking according to the ways of the world, but you were walking according to the prince of the power of the air, the spirit that works in the children of disobedience."* In other words, prior to becoming a Christian there was a spirit working in you that was leading you into the world system. In that world system you were sinning, living outside of God's purposes and you needed to be made alive. The prince of the power of the air was leading you in his way of disobedience, and in his ways of orphan-ness.

THE WORLD IS AN ORPHANAGE

When we understand that Satan is an orphan spirit we see that the ways of this world are, in fact, orphan ways. Satan has deceived the whole world. He has led us down the path into *his* value system, so that the whole world system functions in the ways of the orphan. When we define sin as "missing the mark," it is actually missing the Father and living an orphaned life.

Consider what it is like for an orphan to live in an orphanage, and what it is like for a son to live in a good home with loving parents. There is a huge difference between the two.

Let me outline some of the characteristics of orphan-ness. The basic reality of being an orphan is this. An orphan has no name. Often an orphan's name is changed or they are abandoned and no one actually knows their identity. There is no sense of history, no sense of where you come from. There is no sense of your name meaning anything to you. When you are brought up in a good family your name is the name of your father, and his father before that, stretching back into history. Your name is shared by your brothers and sisters and there is a sense of family identity that comes with having the same name. In the world we see people trying to create a name for themselves, trying to become significant, trying to do something that gives them a place in society. Orphan-ness is not just something to do with the world.

It is the fundamental state of the human heart.

Even in the church we see orphan-ness coming to the fore. We see people in ministry trying to create a name for themselves, trying to do "a significant work," wanting to be involved in "significant ministry." I remember having that very ambition myself. The motivation behind this is that if I do something significant it means that *I* am significant. One of the sayings of the world is, "If you want to feel important, start doing something important." That is a characteristic of being an orphan. A son or a daughter finds their significance from the family, from being loved and cherished simply for who they are.

Another thing about orphans is this. Nobody gives them anything. There are no Christmas presents or birthday presents. If there is a present, it has been given to the orphanage and is distributed randomly. Only by chance would you receive something that you actually want. Maybe a little boy would like a sailing boat, but he is given a truck. Just a random gift with no real and personal meaning attached to it. Birthdays or Christmas don't mean anything to an orphan. The lesson learned is this - you don't get anything for nothing. That is one of the hallmarks of this world. You are on your own, no one is going to give you anything, there is no 'free lunch', and so you had better look after 'number one'.

For an orphan there is no inheritance, so you have to fight for whatever you are going to get. Don't let anyone take it off you, for you can be sure they will try to! That is life in an orphanage. The little boy gets his food taken from him by the bigger boys. The world works this way. Just look at our financial systems. They say, "It's just business, it's not personal" but it is *very* personal for the person on the losing side. An orphan finds it very difficult to be generous because he feels that no one will ever give him anything and if he gives something away it cannot be made up again. A son, on the other hand, has a different view, "My father is very generous and extremely wealthy and he gives good gifts."

The systems by which this world is governed are orphan systems. For example, did you know that democracy is not the Kingdom of God? Democracy may be the best way for orphans to govern orphans in a fallen world but it is still an orphaned system. It is not how God governs His realm. Sadly, many churches are run on the principles of democracy. If you have a church leadership that has an orphan heart, the whole ministry will have a sense of orphan-ness about it. It permeates everything.

Take another example: Capitalism. Capitalism may be the best way that we know for orphans to trade with orphans, but it is certainly not a system based on justice. It is based on orphan values of buying and selling for profit – and as much profit as possible regardless of what is just and fair. The Kingdom of God is different. The Kingdom of God works on the principle of giving away *everything* that you have - and *receiving* everything from God. If someone compels you to go one mile with him, go further. If someone hits you on one cheek, turn the other. If somebody takes your shirt, give him your coat as well.

I am not speaking against business. I am not speaking against making a profit. This is the way the world runs and we need to function within it, but we also need to realize that this is not the way of the Kingdom of God. The Kingdom of God has a different set of values, and as much as we are able, we need to function within God's kingdom, to operate on His principles. Some churches operate their whole budget on the principles of capitalism and it ties them down! God can go far beyond what we think, and if we limit our thinking to what can be done within the system of capitalism then we are limiting what God can do. But when we believe for God's provision in *His* financial systems we are moving out of orphan-ness and into sonship!

The difference between non-Christianity and Christianity is the difference between orphan-ness and sonship.

AN IMAGINARY JOURNEY

I want to take you on a little imaginary journey with me. I want you to try and imagine what it must have been like when Adam was created. We only have a few words in Genesis chapter 3. It says, *"God formed the man from the dust of the ground, breathed into his nostrils the breath of life, and man became a living being."* Imagine if you were an angel watching God create the whole universe. What would this have looked like?

I have often wondered why God did not make man on the first day, so that man could watch Him create everything. That would have been extraordinary, wouldn't it? Why did God wait until the afternoon of the sixth day to create man? The only reason I can come up with is because *He didn't want man to know Him as a working father.* If man had witnessed the act of creation, it may well have instilled in him a striving to work and accomplish. We are made for God's rest and unless we come into a place of rest within ourselves our relationship with God will be hindered. That is why the Scripture says, *"Be still and know that I am God."* (Psalm 46:10).

God formed man. He spoke everything else into being by a word of command, but He formed man, scraping together the dust. There must have come a moment when the angels gasped in surprise as it began to dawn on them that God was making a copy of Himself. It was a perfect creation.

As He was forming this man, there came a time when the body was finally completed. A perfectly formed adult male body but as yet without life. God then breathed into the man's nostrils. You have to get very close to someone to breathe into the nostrils. If you were watching this, what would it look like? *It would look as if God was kissing Adam.*

When a mother holds her newborn child there is a look of absolute wonder and awe on her face. All the pains of childbirth are forgotten, and love, tenderness and amazement are fused together in her expression. I don't think there is any woman that didn't have this sense when she gave birth to her first child. She knows that an amazing miracle has taken place.

God the Father is the prototype parent of all time. He is the ultimate parent and we are copies of Him. When He was breathing into Adam's nostrils He was bringing a son to birth. I imagine that this was one of the most incredible moments in history. If you were watching this you would have seen all of the love and tenderness of the Father in His face.

But what would you see if you were watching Adam? You would see his chest rise and fall with its first breath as the lungs inflated. Then the heart would start to beat. You would see a sudden wave of colour go through the body, as blood starts to pump through the muscles, the tissue, and the skin. Everything in the body would start to function. Maybe as the muscles started to get oxygen, there would be little movements of the fingers, the toes, and the eyelids. Things would start to move because the body is coming alive. Not only is the body coming alive but the brain would be starting to become operative. What would it be like for the mind to be working but have nothing to think about? And the memory would become operative but have no memories! Nothing at all! His personality would be there but as yet there would be no input. Like a computer turned on but with no operating system. It is just blank.

Then the moment arrived when Adam received his first input. What do you think that moment was? What happened to cause him to get his first input? I believe that it was the moment that he opened his eyes. When he opened his eyes what do you think he was looking at? Love is expressed through touch, through the voice and through the eyes. The eyes are a window to the soul.

So Adam was beginning to open his eyes. Do you think the Father had gone off to read the newspaper, watch TV or play football? Never! He was intently loving His son as He was bringing him into existence. God is not a part-time father. He is there all the time. *We* can be preoccupied with other things, but He has nothing else to be occupied with. We are it! When Adam opened his eyes, he was under a "Niagara Falls" of the love of the Father. *He was receiving all of the love that there is in the entire universe.* What a stupendous thought! I cannot imagine what it was like for him, that the very first thing he ever experienced was the total love of Almighty God. Adam knew that he was totally and utterly loved by God.

I thought I was the only one who had thought of this but one day I realized that Paul the apostle had also seen it. When the true import of this verse suddenly dawned on me I thought,

"Paul, you old rascal! You knew this too!" Listen to what he says,

"I pray that you, being rooted and grounded in love, may have power together with all the saints to grasp how wide and long and high and deep is the love of Christ and know His love that passes understanding, that you may be filled to all the fullness of God." (Ephesians 3:14-19)

Rooted and grounded in love. The very foundation of Adam's life was *rooted* and *grounded* in love. Isn't that wonderful? The inheritance of every Christian is to have our eyes opened to see the incredible love that the Father has for us. This is not an extra add-on to Christianity. This is the very foundation! This is not a new book on the bookshelf, so to speak. This is the bookshelf itself! It is not some new experience added onto my other life experiences. This is the basis for the whole lot!! The foundational issue, through which I interpret everything, is that *the Father loves you.*

A man came to me after a meeting some years ago and said, "James, you say that the Father's love is the foundation, but really... the Cross is the foundation, isn't it?" I had never been asked this question before and had not previously thought about it. But in a split second I saw something and I replied, *"The Cross is an expression of the Father's love. The Father's love is not an expression of the Cross."*

Let me put it like this. When you are born again you dive into the well of salvation, encountering the love of Jesus. You dive further in, and you get washed in the blood! You dive further in and He becomes your Lord! You go in deeper and you get filled with the Holy Spirit! You go in further, you are able to move in miracles. You go in further still and you come into ministry and anointing! You go deeper and deeper into justification and sanctification. Then you get to the very bottom of the well, from where *everything* springs. The love of the Father. This is it! He is the Source. His love is the love before all other loves.

PARADISE

Adam became rooted and grounded in love from the very moment that he opened his eyes. Then God created a wife for him. She didn't have another name at that point. They were both called Adam. Love is oneness. Adam (and Eve) had this oneness, just as we also desire to be totally one together. God had created a wonderful environment, which He placed them in.

Adam (and Eve) lived in this garden, totally saturated in the love of the Father. He communed with them every day. We need to understand that God's relationship with Adam was that of a father and son. Scripture calls Adam "the son of God". I have tried to imagine what their life was like but I cannot comprehend it. They would have lived in continual peace. A peace *deeper* than peace. There wouldn't even be a word for peace because there was no alternative. They lived in complete and utter joy. You could have sat down with them and tried to explain the concept of insecurity and they would not have been able to grasp what you were talking about. Fear was completely outside of their frame of reference. This life in the Garden of Eden was innocent but in another sense it was the epitome of maturity. We aspire to that which they had naturally.

We know that Satan set a trap for them and when Satan set this trap he set it well. As a young man I spent some time as a trapper, selling animal skins to make a living. I set many traps in the forest and I know only too well that you have to make them look attractive. You won't catch anything if a trap looks dangerous to the animal that you are trying to catch. It has to look *better* than normal and appear more attractive than the ordinary. Then the prey will catch itself by its own actions.

The first part of Satan's trap was to promise the woman that if she ate from the tree she would be like God. Eve *loved* God. How many of us have prayed that God would make us like Jesus. Why do you pray this? Because you love Him! Love wants to be like and to be incorporated into what it loves. Of course she was interested in Satan's promise. She wanted to be like her Father. She *loved* God.

Then Satan showed her that the fruit was beautiful. One thing I know is that women love beauty. I have stayed in places where there were only men in the house and the house had no beauty, it was just functional. Women love beauty.

Eve looked at the fruit and saw that it was beautiful. She saw that it was good for food and nurture. Nurture can be expressed in many ways, but one of the most common ways is through the creation and provision of good food. It can be an expression of love, care and nurture for the family. Eve reached out, took the fruit and ate it. When she ate the fruit what happened? *Nothing at all.*

Adam and Eve were so united that they couldn't even sin individually. It wasn't until *he also* ate that the eyes of both of them were opened and the trap was sprung...BANG! There was no going back. They couldn't escape. The consequences were set in concrete. I don't believe they really had any idea what the consequences were going to be. They knew that if they ate of the fruit they would die, but that's probably the least of the consequences as far as they were concerned.

The oneness between them was gone. *"And Adam called his wife's name Eve, because she was the mother of all living."* (Genesis 3:20). This is where Eve gets a separate name. They became two, when previously they had been one. C. S. Lewis remarked that a sword came between the sexes that day, a sword of enmity between the male and the female, which has yet to be restored. God then made tunics of skin and clothed them. Now they witnessed blood being shed. *"Then the Lord God said, 'Behold the man has become like one of us, to know good and evil. And now, lest he put out his hand and take also of the tree of life, and eat, and live forever'..."* (v.22). Then He banished them from the garden.

Caught in the trap, sin now became their master. The problem with sin is that it takes hold of you and you cannot escape by yourself. Sin masters you. The only way that the power of sin can be broken is through the blood of Jesus. You cannot break the power of sin by deciding to live differently, but when the blood of Jesus is applied, you are set free from the grip of sin. Adam and Eve stepped into sin but the blood of Jesus had not yet been provided.

Two terrible options

God had an incredible decision to make. Remember that He loved them and wanted only the best for them but now they have taken a path where there are only two possibilities. He could either send them away or leave them in the garden to live forever as sinners.

God was looking at Adam and Eve as the weight of sin descended upon them. They were now going to descend deeper into despair, carrying an ever-increasing burden of guilt. Their personalities would rot away on the inside, caught up in greed, insecurity and fear. The only thing that I can think of, which gives some idea of what this was like, would be the character Gollum, in the film *Lord Of The Rings*. That creature got hold of something powerfully evil. He couldn't let it go, couldn't stop chasing it even though it was destroying him from the inside out. He became a grotesque, wormlike creature, degraded from his original sense of being, and that degradation was continually having an effect on him.

I believe, that as God looked upon Adam and Eve, He realized that they had already begun a process of degradation. And the heart of the Father said, "We cannot allow this to go on forever! Ten thousand years from now they will still be alive and *still degrading*! We cannot allow them to keep eating from the Tree of Life. We need to banish them from the garden. We must stop them having access to the tree!" So He told them, "It's over. You must go!"

How Adam and Eve must have felt when they heard those words is beyond imagination. They couldn't blame God for their predicament. The fact that they had brought it upon themselves only made the despair worse. God came to them as a loving Father. He was not banishing them out of retribution or punishment. Sending them away was choosing the lesser of two evils. When He banished them, Adam and Eve were probably the most broken-hearted people that the world has ever seen.

There are two different things that determine how much pain you experience when someone breaks your heart. Firstly, the greater the love that you have known the greater the pain will be. Adam and Eve had been loved by the greatest love in the universe!

Secondly, if your heart has been broken previously, you generally hold something back the next time. Previous to this, Adam and Eve had never *felt* any pain. They didn't know what pain was. And now, I believe, they were experiencing the greatest emotional pain that anyone had ever felt. They were the saddest and most despairing people that the world has ever seen. Now He pushed them towards the gate out of the garden. It seems like Adam and Eve couldn't make their legs carry them out of the garden and the Father had to physically force them out. He did not do it to punish them. He did not do it because He was rejecting them. He did it *because He loved them.*

God has never done anything that was not an expression of His love and He pushed them out *because* He loved them. I can imagine them dragging their feet, trying to prolong the moments in the garden because for the first time they were starting to experience fear. What would it be like out there? What did He mean that the ground would bring forth thorns and thistles and they would have to work by the sweat of their brow? It meant that He was no longer going to provide! Everything they needed was in the garden! How would they live? They would have to build a different life for themselves. They would never see Him like this anymore. Life as they knew it was over!

HUMAN RACE BECOME ORPHANS

As He was driving them out of the garden, what was really happening was that He was pushing them out of being able to experience His love. They would never experience His love again. Sin always creates separation and now their sin separated them from Him. They must have known as they left the garden that the relationship as it once was had ended. In leaving the garden they were leaving the environment of the Father's love and becoming more like the one cast out of heaven. They were becoming fatherless. The whole human race, including you and I, were in them as they were going out of the garden. *In them the whole human race was becoming orphaned.*

Something even more sinister was happening to compound their misery. The one who was cast to earth like a lightning bolt began to create a deception. An unholy alliance began to develop between the orphan spirit cast out of heaven and this orphan-hearted man and woman who were now totally ignorant of how to live outside the garden. So Satan began to lead the human race in a deception that continues right down through history to this day. We have all walked in his ways, as Ephesians 2: 2 says. The world has become an orphan society. Being saved, filled with the Holy Spirit and knowing Jesus intimately will not change this. Only a Father can eliminate orphan-ness!!

For a long time I never even thought about what it must have been like for God. He loved them with a parental love and He knew what would happen. He knew that greed would now take hold of the human heart and each person would turn against the other. He could see the sword between the sexes, the invisible barrier between the man and his wife as they left the garden. They were now orphans in the fullest sense of the word.

Some years ago I was in St Petersburg in Russia. It was November and bitterly cold. As I was out walking one evening a little boy, about nine years old, ran past me. He was wearing nothing but cotton shorts and a short-sleeved cotton shirt. He had bare feet, dirty legs and uncut hair and carried a little bag of sticks over his shoulder. I presume that he was going to light a fire somewhere to keep warm. As he ran past, he stopped and looked back over his shoulder at me. I will never forget the image of his face. It was like seeing the face of a middle-aged man on a young boy! The look on his face said, "What are *you* going to do to me?" Then he turned and carried on running. There are many children like that all over the world. There is so much suffering in the world. Suffering beyond what we can imagine.

The Father knew what it would be like, as He watched Adam and Eve go out into this orphaned life. But He also knew this was better than the alternative, which was to live forever in continual degeneration. I believe that a great cry began to rise up in the Father's heart at that moment. An agonized cry. One thing that I know as a father is this. When my children suffer, I would rather it was me. It is more difficult to see your children suffering than to suffer yourself. It is almost intolerable to see your children suffer and not be able to do anything about it. And here is a Father sending His children out, knowing the suffering that will inevitably come. I believe that a cry rose up from the depths of His being. As the world went on and the suffering increased, that cry came more and more intense. He could see all of His children, the whole human race, in a life of suffering. His fatherly heart reached out to them, knowing they would soon forget that He even existed and that He loved them.

THE FATHER'S RESCUE PLAN

Out of His heart of absolute compassion, He sent people to tell them of His love. He sent lawgivers and judges, He sent kings and priests to express His heart and to show a way to live free of all the suffering. He called forth a nation of people to be a witness but all of this was inadequate. The whole human race was descending into an orphan life of suffering, experiencing extraordinary levels of loneliness and brokenness. He saw His children suffer and a great cry was welling up within Him. He sent prophets. He sent mothers of Israel. He sent psalmists and poets who could eloquently speak His words. Not one of them could perfectly express His heart. Not one!

Finally He sent His own Son, who would be the perfect representation of Himself, His exact image - His Son, who would not only say what He wanted to say but would say it *exactly the way He wanted it said.* He sent Jesus! Jesus the Son came into the world, totally disconnected from its orphan system, and began to live a life as a Son. He was free of the orphan deception that infected the whole human race. He came in as a Son! His words, which came from being fathered by a perfect Father, amazed the world. He, free of the effect of sin, was able to extend that freedom to others. He dispensed His freedom from sickness, and His freedom from Satan. He could reassure a sinner that their sins were forgiven. He commanded the lame to rise up and walk. He spat on the eyes of the blind and they went away seeing. He came to earth totally free of the orphaned fallen nature of the world to show us what the Father is like, to restore to the world the knowledge that *the Father is loving us.*

In the last days, before He was killed by the world, He was *finally* able to say what had been boiling in His Father's heart, like a volcano, for generations. He was *finally* able to express what His Father wanted Him to express. This cry that was in the Father's heart from the moment Adam and Eve went out of the garden into a fatherless life, deceived by the Orphan Spirit who was thrown out of heaven in the ages past.

Finally Jesus was able to express straight from the Father's heart, the words that the Father told Him to say, saying it the way that His Father wanted Him to say it:

"*I will not leave you as orphans, but I will come to you!!*"

As the Father saw them going out of the garden into orphan-ness, He had to stay behind. But He sent His Son to break down everything that stands between Him and us, and makes the promise, "*I will be a Father to you and you will be My sons and daughters, says the Lord God Almighty!*" (*2 Cor 6:18*). This orphan-ness that is on the whole human race cannot be cast out. It is not in itself demonic. It is the state of the *human* heart. But when the human heart meets the Father it is an orphan no more. And its orphan ways will begin to disappear.

Jesus is not the doorway to get *to* heaven. *He is the door for the Father to come to us!* The curtain in the temple that was torn from the top to the bottom wasn't so that we could go in. *It was torn apart so that He could come out!* He pulled it apart and came out, and in that moment the whole religious edifice collapsed! The kingdom of Israel was gone. Before forty years had passed the temple was destroyed and the royal line of David had vanished! Now the Father comes out of the temple to be a father to the whole world!

The gospel is simply this. It is about a Father who lost His kids and who wants them back.

He sent His Son to bring us home. He said, "Son, go and bring them home. Whoever wants to come, bring them home!" The work of the Spirit of God is to bring us out of orphan-ness and back into sonship. Jesus came as the Son to become the Way to the Father. As you become a son, you can know the Father more and more. That is what Christianity is! Isn't it wonderful? I can hardly believe that He is so good! He is intent on fathering us and banishing our orphaned ways. He is bringing us, His kids, home again to be with Him.

CHAPTER 7

The Secret of Sonship

~

Since I was a young Christian I have been told that I have to mature and grow up. In our Christianity we are trying to become strong, educated, competent, and confident – whereas the Lord is trying to bring us down to childlikeness. In the world you need to become educated to survive and be successful but in the realm of God's rule we need to become as little children. For years, I was trying to do all this hard work until I discovered what it was *really* about.

The Lord has radically changed our whole perspective of the Christian life. When Denise and I were in our thirties we were pastoring a small church in a town in New Zealand. It was our second time of pastoring a church and we were kept very busy. We would spend our evenings and every weekend counselling people. At one point we hadn't been to bed before midnight for two weeks in a row. We also had a vision to build a ministry centre. A friend had been given over one hundred acres and we had moved there to help him build it. We were building houses, installing power lines and sewage systems, as well as upgrading the country road that accessed the site.

Then the Lord spoke to us about building a large eight-bedroom house there. We prayed in the quarter million dollars that it cost to build the house. In addition to this, I was beginning to get invitations to speak outside of New Zealand, so for four years we were extremely busy doing the work of the Lord. From the moment we woke up until we went to sleep at night (and then we were praying for dreams in the night) we were living, eating, breathing and sleeping the Kingdom of God. We were doing everything that we could, endeavouring to do God's work.

Then suddenly a change happened. One morning, I was waiting by the front door for Denise to come down the stairs, so that we could go to church. When she reached the bottom of the stairs she suddenly sat down and began to weep. Anyone who knows Denise knows that she does not cry for nothing. If she was crying, there must be something *seriously* wrong. Had there been a telephone call bringing bad news? She was crying so hard that she couldn't tell me what she was crying about. I kept asking her, "What's wrong?" but she couldn't talk. All she could say finally was, *"I just cannot face those people one more time."*

BURNING OUT

We were emotionally exhausted after seventeen years of serving the Lord full steam. We were living, eating and breathing ministry life. I was teaching in YWAM schools, we were praying for lots of money for different projects, we had speaking engagements in

South East Asia, Korea, the U.S. and Canada as well as the South Pacific Islands. We were putting our whole effort into serving the Lord and suddenly we hit the wall.

This happened in 1988. I decided that we couldn't stay in the ministry with Denise like this. At the time I thought that I was doing fine. I had invitations to speak at four YWAM schools in Australia, so we told our church that we were going to take a six-month break, fulfill our commitments in Australia and then take some time out. As soon as we got to Australia, however, *I* started crying! I would sit on the sofa for hours at a time, staring at the floor with tears streaming down my face. We were emotionally exhausted.

Around that time, Ken Wright and his wife Shirley came to see us. He was the man who had baptized me, one of the men that I thought I could tell the Lord I was a son to. As they were leaving to go home, Ken got into the car, then he wound the window down a couple of inches to say something. It was a good thing that he did this because what he said made me feel like punching him. With a glint in his eye, he said to me, "Of course you realize, don't you James, that only your flesh can burn out." And we *were* burnt out, completely exhausted.

When I heard Ken say those words, everything in me rose up in anger, "I have not been working in the flesh! We have been praying for *everything* to move in the power of the Spirit, seeking to do everything by the power of God!" How could he say that? The problem was, his statement was absolutely inarguable. There was no way that I could say I was exhausted if it was all the Lord's work and all by His strength. If you get burned out, it is a clear indicator that a lot of *"you"* has been involved in the work. That was a hard fact for me to face. Everything in my life, as far as serving the Lord went, was motivated by the desire that the Lord would move by *His* power and by *His* Spirit. We always sang that song, *"It's not by might, not by power, but by my Spirit, saith the Lord."* I discovered that a lot of people sang the song and would then go out and use their own strength and their own power to do God's work. Singing the song didn't make a lot of difference.

And so, with all of our busyness, we had become completely exhausted. We were out of ministry for two years. We were out of everything. We were almost out for the count. Denise thought that we would never come back into any form of ministry again, and I had no idea what I would do with the rest of my life if I didn't. For two years we did very little. We tried to do some jobs, but the simplest things were hard to do. To think in a logical sequence for half an hour was very difficult. A simple task like mowing the lawn was an extreme effort for me. I would regularly feel the need to sleep after mowing the lawn. Not because I was physically tired but because I was mentally exhausted from the effort.

Through that whole experience, I began to re-examine a lot of things about the Christian life. I had always made it a priority to fulfill every obligation and duty, in my private quiet times, my preparation of sermons and visiting the sick. When I was a pastor a constant stream of people would come into my office to share their problems with me. They would go out without their problem but they had left their problems *with me*, and now *I* was carrying the problems while they felt better. This kept accumulating over the years until I couldn't handle it any more. I began to think that there had to be a better way.

Pressure to grow up

After a couple of years, I received an invitation to be the pastor of a little charismatic Baptist church in Auckland. I went to visit them and told them about my state of health. I told them what my doctor and close friends said about me. They responded, "We won't ask you to do a lot. If you could just put in a couple of days a week, that would be a good start." They were so gracious to us. We spent the next seven years there and they healed us and we healed them because they had been through a difficult time after their pastor and eldership had walked out on them. We were able to focus the people back onto the Lord rather than the issues, and the Lord healed us all throughout that time together.

In 1994, I heard about the Toronto outpouring so I went to Canada and was deeply moved by what God was doing there. I had the feeling that new life was being breathed into me. I could sense the blessing of the Lord and felt that we were starting off a new day. Then, in 1997, we purchased a round-the-world air ticket to travel with Jack Winter and see what God might do through us. We didn't unpack our suitcases for the next four and a half years and we are still travelling in this ministry, living in the new day.

When I first became a Christian, the predominant message that I was taught went something like this,

"Now that you have become a Christian, you must grow up in the Lord. Now you have to be mature. You've got to get the victory, brother! Whatever it is that comes up, you have to make the breakthrough. You have to seek God and find Him in the midst of the situation and become an overcomer!" etc. etc.

And so there was this continuous kind of pressure to become mature. In those days we sang a particular song, which I hated to sing. A lot of the lyrics were taken from Scripture but there was one line that just distorted the meaning of all the scriptures that were in the song. I apologize to whoever wrote it, but the song was something like this, *"I'm a conqueror, I'm victorious, I'm reigning with Jesus. I'm seated in heavenly places with Him."* Now, that's all scriptural. But then it comes to this line that I couldn't sing. It said, *"I know no defeat, only strength and power."* I know that is supposed to be a positive confession but if I had to say it, it would be a lie because I had known a lot of defeat in my life and not just strength and power.

The message was constantly reinforced,

"You have to speak positively. You can't allow any negative thoughts in because you are an overcomer! You must walk in faith and hold on to the victory. You must get your act together, become competent and faith-filled. You must know the Word, hear all the messages, listen to all the preachers, and read all the books. You need to become the Got-It-All-Together Christian, the mature Man of God!"

There was a saying, "When you become a Christian, you really have to get your act together!" I realize now that even if you actually *do* get your act together, it's still just an act! A lot of our positive talk is just bravado rather than faith. If we can be honest about where we are at instead of denying the realities we can gain a lot of ground spiritually. Many things we were taught to do were a kind of denial and denial is not victory.

THE KNIGHT ON THE WHITE HORSE

Some years ago I had a vision that was a life-changing encounter.

In this vision, I was standing in an ancient forest. I knew it was an ancient forest because the trees were huge oak trees with big boughs spreading out wide. It reminded me of Sherwood Forest from the story of Robin Hood. I was standing there on the grassy forest floor and, as I looked, I suddenly saw that I was standing on an ancient road that was no longer used and was overgrown with grass. I could see the outline of it winding away through the trees. As I stood there, I noticed that something was coming through the trees towards me.

As it came closer, I could see that it was a white horse and mounted on the horse was a medieval knight. His armour was brilliant, translucent white or silver. The knight was holding a sword in the air showing the flat of the blade rather than poised to attack. His other arm was outstretched with an open hand. The strange thing was that he wasn't holding any reins! As he approached, I could see that the horse was *dancing*. A few steps forward and a few steps back. A few steps this way and a few steps that way. It repeated this motion over and over again. There was no hurry. The knight was just sitting there with his hands raised, holding up the sword.

The knight slowly approached me on his dancing horse and my eyes began to recognize more movements. Out of the darkness of the forest, people were coming towards the road. The glow of light that surrounded the horse and rider was reaching out into the darkness of the forest. Some people were weeping and some were laughing. Others were wounded and they were crawling into the light and being filled with joy. Some were dancing like little children, holding hands and dancing in circles. Some were kneeling beside the road with their hands raised as the knight went past, worshipping the Lord. The knight was not the Lord but he was carrying the glory of the Lord and it was pulsating out from him into the darkness of the forest.

With a sudden start I realized that I was standing right in the middle of the road. But I had nothing to fear and I didn't feel that I was supposed to stand aside to let them pass. I stood there and the horse came right up to me and stopped. The knight had the visor down on his helmet so that his face was hidden. It appeared that he wasn't interested in me nor did he take any notice of me. He just sat there without making any movement. Then I felt intuitively that I was invited to put my foot into the stirrup where the knight's foot was. So I put my foot in the stirrup on top of his armoured foot and pulled myself up to stand alongside him. He had not changed his position at all. His sword was still raised and his hand outstretched. I looked at him but I couldn't see his face because the visor was down and the slit in the visor was so narrow that nothing could be seen behind it.

I reached out and lifted the visor to see his face. But when I lifted the visor, there was no face there! No face at all. So I took the helmet right off and to my shock there was no head! Then I looked down into the neck of the armour and sitting down inside the armour there was a little boy – just a little boy! The little boy had a great big smile on his face, as if to say, *"This is the joke of the century! I'm just sitting on this horse and we're dancing and all of these things are happening around me and people are coming out to the Lord, people are getting touched and saved and healed and blessed and everything is happening - and they think I'm a big knight of God. But I'm just a little boy!"* When I saw that, and saw that little boy's face with the big smile, for the first time in my life I began to understand what Christian ministry was all about.

THE CHURCH IS A PARTY

Over the years, the church has been described in many different ways. It has been described as an army. Somebody once wrote a book called *The Bride with Combat Boots*. Even though I have never read the book, I must admit that I don't like the title. Imagine going to a wedding and the music begins for the bride to walk up the aisle…Here comes the bride…clomp, clomp, clomp, clomp. The wedding guests turn around to see her walking up the aisle, her combat boots thumping on the stone floor. I cannot bring myself to believe in that description of the bride.

We have thought that the church is an army and everyone has to get in step and march with military precision. The church is a more varied expanse of gifting and freedom than anything we have ever dreamed of. The church was never intended to make everyone the same. It is a place where individuality can be fully expressed in perfect synthesis with others. The church is a symphony of giftings under the direction of the Holy Spirit. Some have described the church as a hospital, where we all lie in beds until we get fixed up. That is a dominant idea in church circles but I have discovered the truth. Do you know what the church *really* is? *The church is a party.*

As a young Christian I was constantly exhorted to go out and save the world. The world does need to be saved, of course! The answer is Jesus. However, it is not my knowledge and my understanding (*even* of Christianity) that saves the world. When I came out of that period of burnout people would come to see me with their problem. As I listened to them, I would keep repeating in my mind, "This is not my problem. I do not have to fix this." I would pray that the Lord would help them and minister to them, because I couldn't take that burden on myself. There are things that are going on in our life that are primarily between the Lord and us. People can help you but they cannot carry you. So I learned how to keep from being burdened down with these things and be like a little child.

CHILDLIKENESS

I have discovered a particular characteristic of godly people. The most wonderful and Christlike people are also the most childlike. Jack Winter was incredibly childlike. He just believed the Bible, and as a result he saw God do many amazing things.

Jack had an intercessor called Amy who prayed for him and who subsequently interceded for us. She was in her eighties when I first met her. She came to New Zealand, and interceded for me for two weeks, for eight hours a day in tongues. That was her assignment. She brought a friend with her and they would go into this little room, close the door and we would hear the most incredible noises coming out of that room. They would pray with great authority. However, when she stopped praying and came out of the room to sit with us for lunch, she was like a little three year-old girl! She was joking all the time. She was so funny to be with and her laughter had an innocent purity with no sophistication whatsoever. Just like a little child has no idea how to be sophisticated or dignified, neither did she. She was like a little girl.

We have been told so much that we need to grow up. We have been told that we need to become competent and mature, full of faith and power. We have been told that we need to learn all the lessons and accumulate knowledge so that we can always give answers to people's questions. Preachers would often say to me, "If the church was really doing its job, we would be doing this and that because it is our responsibility to fix this world." Do you know where He found us? He found us in drains, under hedges and down alleyways - some literally. We had broken and messed up lives. We are not the noble of this world. We are not the ones who have it all together. We are the ones without hope, who couldn't do anything right. He found me under a tree in the wilderness somewhere. I don't know why He chose me. I'm the dregs of society. Why did He come and find me?

The whole purpose of man is to *worship God and enjoy Him forever*, says the Westminster Confession. That is enough. We don't need anything more. This applies to ministry as well as our personal lives. Christianity is not a path to competency but *a path to childlikeness*. The more childlike we become, the closer we are to Him. And the closer we are, the more childlike we become. Do you think Jesus said to us, "*Unless you become as a little child you cannot enter the Kingdom of God,*" but there was a different way for Him?

Children know how to enjoy life. Who has the most joy? A lawyer or a child? Who is the best at laughing from their belly? An architect, a policeman or a little girl? It is always a child. Why? Because they aren't caught up with all the competency issues of life. They will laugh and laugh at something that we don't even smile at. They have an incredible capacity to simply enjoy the present moment. In many cases Christianity as we know it has added to the seriousness of our lives. We can walk a tightrope of the fear of not doing things correctly and not living right. No wonder the non-Christian person looks at us and thinks, "*I do not want to be like that!*"

JESUS IS CHILDLIKE

Jesus Himself was extremely childlike. Matthew 11:25 says, "*At that time, Jesus answered and said, "I thank You, Father, Lord of heaven and earth that You have hidden these things from the wise and the prudent and have revealed them to babes."*

It took me many years to realize that Jesus is actually talking about Himself here. What are "these things" that He is talking about here? He is talking about the things that He has been teaching in the preceding few chapters. If they were not revealed to the wise and prudent who *were* they revealed to? *They were revealed to Jesus.* He was the one who was teaching them. *The Father taught Him these things because He had the heart of a little child.* He said *"My doctrine is not My own."* (John 14:10) In other words, "I haven't got this theologically figured out. I don't have opinions on all of the doctrinal issues."

He also said, *"The Son can do nothing of Himself."* (John 5:19) He didn't say, "The Son will do nothing *by* Himself," which is how many of us read that scripture. He said: *"The Son can do nothing OF himself."* In other words, "There is nothing in Me that can do these things that I am doing or teach these things that I am teaching. The miracles that I do are happening *through* Me, not of Me. The words that I speak are not My words. It is the Father living in Me who is doing it all."

He didn't say, "The Son *doesn't want* to do anything of Himself." Nor did He say, "The Son has *chosen not* to do anything of Himself." He said, "The Son *can* do nothing of Himself." What an incredible statement!

I say this with reverence, but Jesus was incredibly incompetent. He wasn't grown-up and mature! He was childlike. So often in the church today we aspire to what is wise and prudent. Jack Winter used to remark that this revelation is often difficult for pastors and leaders to receive. Having been a pastor myself I can well understand the pressures that pastors and leaders are under. Pastors often receive this message as good for the congregation but not applicable to the leadership. Church leaders need to open their hearts to receive what God has for them.

Wisdom is acting correctly in a given situation while prudence is making correct choices for our future good. Often pastors can be focused on trying to do things the right way - "What is the right thing to say, the right way to approach this situation? What is the right way to do this? What do we do in the leaders' meeting? How do we prepare for the next five years?" Slowly it becomes more and more about how to live your life right and how to do "the right thing." Jack believed that the pastors had often become the "wise and prudent" and had closed off the childlike heart.

I am not saying that we shouldn't do these things, but don't assume that it amounts to maturity. When we start to think along the lines of, *"This is what maturity is, now I'm a mature Christian because I do all these things,"* what happens is that having wisdom and prudence becomes our life goal, which actually acts as a hindrance to receiving revelation. Revelation is given to a *childlike* heart. I believe that this is one of the reasons why the Body of Christ in the last century has made such little inroads into real revelation and intimacy with God. We have been focusing on becoming wise and prudent, when the Lord is actually leading us on the path to become a little child.

KNOWING EVERYTHING IS NOT HAPPINESS

A few years ago I was in Holland in a place called Vlissingen. While I was having coffee with my host one morning he said to me, "James, I've discovered something. *Knowing everything doesn't make you happy.*" That statement affected me tremendously. From the time I first became a Christian it was drummed into me that I had to know everything, and, to be a Christian leader, I had to have an opinion on everything. I had to know what every Scripture really meant or at least be informed on all the different opinions that are out there. The pressure was on me to *know everything*.

A little later, while still in Holland, I was the speaker at a men's camp and was sharing a room with a big Dutchman who spoke with a booming voice. We have subsequently become good friends. On Sunday, after the last session had finished, we were sitting on our bunk beds waiting to be driven back to Amsterdam. As we sat there he asked me a question about a leadership issue, or something to do with Christian ministry. I replied, "Oh. I don't know." His eyes perceptively widened, then he fell back on the bed *bellowing* with laughter. The whole bed was shaking as he laughed. After a couple of minutes, he looked at me, "*You don't know?*" I said, "No, I don't." and he fell back on the bed again, rolling around in laughter. I just sat there, amazed at his reaction. Finally he sat up again, "James, you are the preacher. *You have to know!*" You see, that is the pressure that comes upon us. The pressure to accumulate the knowledge, to get the wisdom, and to become the expert.

PAUL SIMON'S SONG

After Denise and I suffered burnout we went to Australia to fulfill a prior speaking engagement to some YWAM schools. It was a horrendous time in our life. We were totally exhausted, but the Lord helped us in all the things that we needed to do. We were driving through the outback from Adelaide to Brisbane and we had passed through a town in far western New South Wales called Bourke. There is a saying that if you are "back of Bourke" it means that you are in the real outback! Very few Australians even get that far into the outback. So we were driving along these roads where you can drive for twelve hours without a change in the scenery.

As we drove we were listening to Paul Simon's album *Graceland* on the car stereo. A song came on with lyrics about a character called Fat Charlie The Archangel. It went like this, *"Fat Charlie the Archangel sloped into the room. He said 'I have no opinion about this. And I have no opinion about that."* Suddenly Denise and I began laughing. An "archangel" doesn't even have an opinion! It's OK not to know! Even if you're an archangel! As we began to laugh, the pressure to grow up and be strong, to be mature and to have it all together began to dissipate. After striving for years to become knowledgeable, the idea that an "archangel" didn't actually have an opinion was a great relief.

"Busy, Busy, Busy"

Often when I go to churches, I will have an opportunity to spend some time with the pastor before the meeting at which I am going to speak. A church has its own culture, just as each nation has its own culture. I visit many different churches, so when I arrive at a place for the first time my spiritual antennae are up, trying to work out what the culture and beliefs are in order to build rapport with them and communicate effectively. Often I will ask the pastor some questions, the answers to which give me a lot of insight. One question that I ask the pastor is, "How is your church going?" Very often, I get the following answer or something to a similar effect,

"Oh, we're very busy. It's all 'GO' here! We've got so much on, the

church is really growing. We've got this conference happening and that speaker coming. We're extending the car park and we need to enlarge the kitchen. We've got outreaches going to Africa this weekend. The youth group is really growing. In fact, it's so big we've got new pastors coming on for youth work. And we've got to get more parking attendants. We're raising money for this and we're raising money for that. We have a new church plant over here and another happening over there. The women's ministry has really taken off and we're making outreaches into the next town."

All I hear is, "Busy, busy, busy." Many pastors think that is what you want to hear. If you are the visiting speaker, they want to give a good impression. When I hear all about the busyness I think, "Uh oh. What's going wrong here?"

Imagine that you went to Jesus one day as He was walking around Nazareth and asked Him, "How's the ministry going, Jesus?"

"Oh, it's busy, busy, busy! We're off to Capernaum this afternoon; we need to organize a boat to pull us out because the crowd is going to be too big. We can't have microphones but we can use the water. And Lazarus just died so I'm supposed to be up in Bethany, and Mary and Martha are really upset. I should have been there days ago but it's been all go, go, go! I've been speaking and teaching all over the place, and I'm working with the disciples, but Peter is a bit of a problem. So I need to get him sorted out. And then I was tied up throwing the moneychangers out of the temple. You know, somebody died and I was kind of waylaid and I had to go to another place and raise someone else from the dead. So that put us behind schedule a little, but we got the lady with the issue of blood fixed and we're on our way – it's all go, go, go! Gotta get these disciples trained."

If you had asked Jesus how His ministry was going, I don't believe that He would have responded with something like that! He would probably have replied with something like, *"Father is really wonderful. We've been seeing Him do some amazing things. We're just along for the ride you know. It's incredible what He is doing. It's not Me, it's Him! He tells Me what to say and I say it. It's incredible to see what happens when I say what He tells Me to say. When I touch people, I see spectacular things happen. We saw this guy with a withered arm the other day and his whole arm was restored. It was just wonderful! This is an amazing time!"*

I believe that He would have been filled with joy. When John the Baptist's disciples came to him with the question, *"Are you the Messiah or are we to wait for another?"* His reply was, *"Go and tell him what you hear and see. The blind are seeing, the lame are walking, the deaf are hearing."* He didn't feel the need to reassure John that He was the Messiah. I believe that He was *really* saying, "What is happening is wonderful. We're not doing anything. God is doing everything. We're just like little kids playing in the mud and it's all fun."

As I stated earlier, I have come to learn that the Kingdom of God is a party. Very often we have turned it into an evangelistic outreach or a cause. We have turned it into something that is serious and heavy. There's never any problem inviting someone to a party but you might have difficulty getting them to come to church.

YOUR WEAKNESS IS YOUR STRENGTH

Paul the apostle knew what it was to live in the paradox of weakness. He talks about it in his second letter to the church at Corinth. Incidentally, I find it very interesting how much Paul talks about himself. It would be a fascinating study to look at the instances in which Paul uses the words "I," "me," "my," or "mine" throughout his writings. Six times in his letters he counsels, "Imitate me." I would suggest that every time Paul talks about himself it is worth taking particular notice. In 2 Corinthians 12:7, Paul begins to talk about himself, saying,

"Lest I should be exalted above measure by the abundance of the revelations, a thorn in the flesh was given to me, a messenger of Satan to buffet me lest I be exalted above measure."

We don't exactly know what the thorn in the flesh was, but what we know for sure is that Paul had a problem. It was not a simple problem either. Some people have joked that the thorn in the flesh was his wife. I don't give any credibility to that! I generally find that husbands are more of a thorn in the flesh to their wives than the other way round. Some people have said that Paul's thorn in the flesh was that he was short in stature because the meaning of his name is "small." For a man of his calibre that would be of little significance. I don't think that being "vertically challenged" would have affected Paul at all. Some people have said that this thorn in the flesh was that Paul was going blind. Now that is a possibility. He said in Galatians 4:15, *"I know that if possible, you would have plucked out your own eyes and given them to me."* He knew their love for him because he had shared the Gospel with them. Whatever the thorn in his flesh was though, he certainly had a problem. What is more, he describes it as being "a messenger of Satan," so it must have been something quite distressing for him.

In the next verse he says,

"Concerning this thing, I pleaded with the Lord three times that it might depart from me."

Now Paul had been through a lot and he had experienced the grace of God in all of it. But whatever this was, it caused him to really plead with God three times, to take it away. This was obviously a very difficult thing to live with. When he asked the Lord to take it away, his request was denied. However, God was saying to him, "My grace is sufficient for you, for My strength is made perfect in weakness."

My strength is made perfect in weakness. The truth is, if you want to have the power of God resting upon you and you are strong in yourself, you actually disqualify yourself from having the power of God on you. The power of God comes upon people who are weak. Paul's strength was not that he had become strong, competent and had all the answers. On the contrary, the grace of God came on him *because* of his weakness. The Lord said, "My grace is sufficient for you for My strength is made perfect in weakness."

What I have discovered is this, if you think that God uses you because you pray a lot, or that He uses you because you have done this or that, *then your heart will take the glory for itself.* You can even say, "I give all the glory to the Lord," but it is not your speech that the Lord takes account of. He looks at your heart. When your heart takes the glory, God will cut off the power. He will not share His glory with anybody. It takes faith to know that there is nothing in us that qualifies us for God to use us. It takes more faith to step out and trust God to use you. It takes much more faith to step out in God when you have an overwhelming sense that there is absolutely nothing in you that is valuable to God.

Be a little child

One more example of Paul's weakness can be seen in 1st Corinthians, Chapter 2. According to scholars, the Corinthian church was the most carnal church of that day. That was their reputation, at any rate. And here is Paul, the top rabbinical student of his day. He was academically brilliant and filled with religious zeal. Now he has had this incredible revelation from the Lord, so much so that he needed a thorn in the flesh to keep him from being exalted in his own heart. Even the apostle Peter didn't understand many of the things that Paul said. He wrote (in 2 Peter 3:16), *"...our beloved brother Paul...has written to you, as also in all his epistles, speaking in them of these things, in which are some things hard to understand."* Peter struggled to understand what Paul was talking about. Paul's depth of revelation was obviously incredible and here he was coming to the Corinthian church to try to sort them out.

In chapter 2 verse 3, he wrote to the Corinthian church, *"I was with you in weakness, in fear and in much trembling."*

He didn't show up at Corinth saying, "I've got this whole church growth system figured out. I know just how to do it. I can come and sort out all your problems. I know what to say to the church leaders and the team. I've had experience and practice. I know the ropes. I'll fix your church in a week - no problem - two weeks at the outside." He didn't say anything like that. He said rather, *"I came to you in weakness and in fear and in much trembling."* He didn't know what to do.

Paul had learned the same secret that Jesus knew. Be a little child. When we think we know how to do it all, we are disqualified.

God comes to us in our weaknesses. You don't need to have it all together to be God's son or daughter. One of Denise's best friends, Katie, gave her testimony in a meeting some years ago and I have never heard such a devastating testimony in my life. The more she shared the more I felt that she was my sister. I had not experienced the same kind of pain but I could relate to the reality of her story. When people give a presentation of strength and how they have it all together, I have absolutely no idea how to relate to that. I know there are times that I *look* like I have it together, and when the anointing comes it looks like I am wearing a suit of armour. It can look like I really am a knight of God. *But take the helmet off and look down the neck hole.*

No longer playing the game

In the past I used to pretend to be a competent person and I learned all these different little tricks to show strength. Then I began to see that my weakness is actually my biggest asset. I was just a hunter who got saved by mistake! It wasn't my fault! A very brave person prophesied over me that I was to become a teacher of the Word. It was the bravest prophecy anyone ever gave if you saw what I looked like that particular day. And I was crazy enough to believe it. So I figured that, if I was going to be a teacher of the Word, I had better start reading it. I have been reading it ever since and now I feel as if I am standing in a river of revelation, knowing full well that it is not because of my competency.

In these recent years of our Christian experience, we have been having the time of our lives. I could only experience that freedom and joy once I was able to release everything that I felt I was supposed to become and just be a little boy in the arms of my Father.

Do you know what the key to this revelation of the Father's love is? Just become a little child. *A little child.* The more that you try to be sophisticated and know it all, read all the Scriptures, listen to the sermons and read all the books; the more you want to be the big, strong, grownup man or woman of God and have that reputation, the less capacity you have to know the Father as a loving Father to *you.*

In my vision of the knight riding out of the forest I felt like a little boy...*but I was sitting on a white horse.* The white horse is the Holy Spirit. And if you are going to sit on that horse you are not allowed to hold on to the reins. You have to go wherever He dances. And it is a dance. God wants to use us. He wants His power to be revealed through us but the paradox is that *your weaknesses are your greatest assets.* Have you got weaknesses in your life? Have you got problems that you can't figure out how to fix? They are your greatest assets. So often we are waiting for God to fix them before He can use us. Let me tell you something. He uses you in the midst of your weakness. The weaker you are, the more He can use you. The greatest handicap is our own strength, our own competency, our accreditation and accomplishment. Being "full of faith and power" and "having it all together" is our greatest hindrance.

If you have your strength, He will let you have the product of your strength. However, if you can be weak you will get the product of His strength and that is infinitely better.

CHAPTER 8

The Glorious Freedom of Sons

~

With all of my heart I desire that you will be helped to open your heart to receive the love of the Father. It is His deepest desire to have His children close to Him, living in that place of intimacy, hidden in Christ in the Father's heart. But that is not all there is to it. There is so much more, a glorious inheritance to be entered into, the inheritance that belongs to the sons and daughters. He is our inheritance, but even more glorious, we are *His* inheritance. Now for the culmination! This is what lies ahead. It is the opening up of the vista that is as wide as eternity itself. So fasten your seatbelt, and get ready for the ride of your life.

The way that I minister has sometimes been very scary. Watchman Nee observed that there are two different ways to speak with anointing. One is to have a message where you know exactly what you are going to share all the way through and then you are able to release anointing into it. The other way is to follow the anointing so that you don't know where you are going or what you are going to say, which is much more scary but also a lot more fun in the sense that you are never sure what the Lord is going to say next. Sometimes I find myself speaking, not knowing what I'm saying, and being surprised by the things that I hear coming out of my own mouth. Very often I find myself saying something and I have absolutely no idea what I'm talking about! This happened one particular time in Germany and, of course, working with an interpreter I had a little more time to pray between sentences. I said something and I didn't know why I said it but I felt that it was the Lord. I was talking about how God loves to come and be a Father to us in all of the everyday things of our lives. He loves to show His love by providing ordinary things like car parking spaces, for instance. As I was preaching this I suddenly heard myself saying, *"But that's not what He's really after!"*

WHAT IS HE REALLY AFTER?

When I said it, I immediately thought, "Well…what *is* He after?" What else could there be? I felt that it was really the Holy Spirit speaking but I hadn't the remotest idea what He was really after! Inside myself I was saying, "Lord, what *are* You really after?" He didn't say anything, so I kept on speaking and said, "He loves to come into our church services and anoint our worship…but that's not what He's really after!" "What *is* He really after?" my heart cried!

My mind was racing ahead and thinking, "What on earth am I going to say?" I felt like I was digging a hole deeper and deeper, and I was not going to be able to get out of it! I had no idea what was going to happen but there seemed to be no other option than to keep talking. So I launched into telling a story about an experience that Denise and I had.

I told the story of when we were in Holland a couple of years back, driving to a railway station in a real hurry. The trains in Holland go right on the minute; they do not delay even for seconds. If you are not there at the exact time you miss the train. So we were driving to the station to catch a train. We had four minutes to park, get out of the car, grab our cases, buy the railway ticket, go to the platform, and get on the train. So we were pushed for time. We came into the carpark and it was full. Not only that, but there were hundreds of bicycles leaning up against the walls of the carpark and we realized that this was a very busy time of the day. We were cruising up and down the aisles of the carpark looking for an empty space but there wasn't one to be seen. It was totally full. So Denise prayed, "Father, would You give us a parking space?" She had started praying as soon as we came into the car park because she figured that she needed to give the Lord time to send someone back to their car. It requires a little bit of time even for God to organize these things.

So as we drove around trying to find a space she added, "Lord, even make somebody feel a *little* bit sick and decide not to go to work today!" Now I don't know about the theology of this but she prayed that anyway as we came to another row of parking spaces - and saw a guy at the far end who had parked his car and was walking straight towards us. Suddenly he stopped, turned around and headed back towards his car. Denise yelled to Vince who was driving, "Follow that man!" So off we went in pursuit. As we came round the corner he got into his car, pulled out and drove away. An empty parking space! We zoomed right in and Denise said, "You can make him feel well now, Lord!" It was the nearest parking space to the station door. We jumped out, grabbed our tickets, hurried along one platform, dragging our suitcases, down the stairs, along another platform, up the stairs again, came out onto the platform where our train was waiting, walked straight through the train door, the doors closed behind us and we were off. We made it – just!

That's who He is. He loves being a father to His kids like that. But, as I was speaking this day, I kept saying, *"But that's not what He's really after!* He loves to anoint our crusades, our outreaches, our missionary endeavours to the nations, *but that's not what He's really after!"* That phrase just kept coming and I could feel the tension building in the room. Everyone was thinking, "What *is* He really after?"…and I didn't know! Finally, as I was saying it again, He showed me.

You see, He loves to come and be a father to us in all of the stuff of our lives, but what He is *really* after is us becoming sons and daughters to Him in all of the stuff of *His* life. He is looking for us to not just know Him as a father in *our* world, but to become sons and daughters to Him in *His* world, in *His* perspective of living.

One thing that I have noticed about fathers and mothers is that they want their children to experience a quality of life similar to *or better* than their own. Whatever their level of education is, they want their children to be educated as much, if not more, than themselves. They always want better for their kids. Let me tell you, God feels the same way about us as His children. He is our Father and His desire is for us to come to be sons and daughters *appropriate to who He is.*

When we first began to hear about the Father's love, we thought it was just for emotional healing. Then we came to realize that there was far more to this than we had ever thought. He pours His love into our hearts and heals us in the traumas of our lives but that's just the starting point. Many of us begin to experience the Father's love and think, "Oh, now I'm all healed up I can go back to what I was doing and carry on as before, because now I can do it as a healed person." The purpose of God is much, much more than that. He wants us to learn to walk continually before Him in weakness. His desire is that we would become accustomed to the same sense of vulnerability and dependence that Jesus walked in. One of the biggest secrets of Christian life is learning to become comfortable with weakness instead of trying to fight it.

Often we will humble ourselves and be weak *in private* in order to be healed but Father wants us to learn to live there. Vulnerability feels risky. God doesn't want us to make a one-off visit to humility, but to *live* there. As we learn to live in that vulnerable place of constantly needing His love and increasingly identifying with the words, "*The Son can do nothing of Himself*," then God can use us. You can reach heights in God that cannot be reached other than by humility. So as we learn to live there, He is able to work with us as His sons and daughters. This is what I have begun to see. The Father wants us to become sons and daughters *appropriate to who He is*.

When I found myself speaking this in Germany that first time, it was the very beginnings of a revelation that not only began to change my life, but my identity. At that time of my life I had been thinking, "Well, we have a relatively successful itinerant ministry, which I'm enjoying more than anything else I have ever done in my life. We have enough to live off. It's working for us in practical ways." I was thinking, "This is it! I'm an itinerant speaker traveling around the world and speaking about the Father; then I go home, have a holiday, and travel again. It's working very well!"

But when I saw that God is calling us to be sons and daughters appropriate to who *He* is, in *His* perspective of the universe - that was when I began to think that I needed to find a direction in life appropriate to a son of God and not just an itinerant speaker. What could I do with my life that would make me to be a son *appropriate* to who my Father is? - Because my Father just happens to be Almighty God! That was when we began to envision this whole dream of seeing the love of the Father go to every stream of Christianity, to every culture, every nation, and every person in the world. And so this whole story began. We began to develop schools in which people could be impacted as deeply as possible with an experience of the Father's love, because once it gets into your heart your whole world changes.

WHAT IS GOD LIKE?

When you begin to consider what it means to be a son or a daughter appropriate to who the Father is it leads to another question. What is my Father really like? What are the big concepts that describe who my Father is? These are the attributes that we need to explore in order to move into a sonship appropriate to who *He* is. What are some of the big words or concepts that describe Him? Let me list some familiar ones that immediately spring to mind. God is Truth, compassionate, relational, Yes! Salvation, faith, hope, joy all describe aspects of His nature. Absolutely! More spring to mind, such as mercy, glorious, holy. Then you could list the "omni's." Omniscient, omnipotent, omnipresent.

As I was thinking about these attributes of God, another word suddenly came to my mind. It was a word that I had never previously considered as describing the nature of God. What is more, I had never heard any Christian speaker using this word either. It was the word "free." God is FREE.

Freedom is probably one of the most precious things to the human heart. We watch films about freedom, read books about emancipation, listen to music that expresses freedom. Why does the character William Wallace in the film *Braveheart* catch our imagination? It is because everything in us responds to a man who would give his life for freedom for himself, freedom for his people and nation. Freedom is probably one of the biggest issues that we face as a human race. More than anything else, people want to be free. The opposite of freedom is slavery. I cannot imagine anything worse than slavery. I would rather be dead! Slavery has to be one of the most cruel things that the human race has ever devised. There is no decision that you can make as an individual, in any way whatsoever. You have no control whatsoever over what you do from one moment to the next. You have no control over what you eat or what clothes you can wear. If you marry, you could end up separated for life if one or both of you are sold in different places. The slavery of children is even worse. It goes against everything that is free within us. There is something in us that tends towards hope, that believes for something better.

Freedom is intrinsic to God's nature and His heart. He is *total freedom*. Freedom is always measured by limitations. Does God have any limitations? He can do anything, can't He? He can create anything He wants. There are no limits to His freedom. Well, there is only one thing He cannot do. He cannot sin. That in itself is not a limitation although I used to think it was, until I understood the nature of sin. People would say to me, "Sin is a terrible, horrible thing. Don't ever do it! God hates it. It's wrong. It's bad. It's evil!" But these explanations didn't satisfy me one bit because there were some behaviours that were labelled as sins that didn't seem to hurt anyone else. What was so terrible and wrong with those particular things? There are many things that are obviously wrong but there were some sins that I honestly couldn't see any harm in. There are some things that we allow in our life because we don't fully understand what is so bad about them or because we can't see the evil in that particular behaviour.

The real problem with sin is *that it binds you to it*. Sin gets hold of you and it *masters* you, *controls* you, *binds* you up, and takes away your freedom. *That* is why sin is so bad. As God said to Cain, "*Sin is at the door and its desire is to master you.*" (Gen 4:7). Sin's desire is always to master us and when we get involved in sin, its chains entangle us and begin to drag us down. The reason why God doesn't want us to sin is not so much because sin is "bad" (so to speak) but because He knows that it will destroy your soul. It will drag you deeper and deeper into bondage from which there is no escape but by the blood of Jesus.

So when we say that God cannot sin it is because *He will not lose His freedom*. He will not be mastered by anything. He will always remain free. I had never realized that freedom was such a big issue for God. What is more, I began to see this every time I read the Bible. Passages such as Romans 8:15, 2 Corinthians 6:18 and Galatians 4:6 all talk about us as sons and daughters of God coming into that same experience of *freedom* that He experiences.

THE FREEDOMS OF THIS WORLD

When we look at freedom from our human perspective, it would seem that those who possess the most freedom in this world are probably the wealthiest. If you have lots of money you can do anything you like. The more money you have the greater freedom you have. Some years ago the actor John Travolta flew into New Zealand in his own Boeing jet, which he piloted himself. He was flying into Auckland airport and as he was coming to the point where he would enter the landing pattern, on a whim he suddenly decided not to land but to fly the length of New Zealand and admire the country first. So he flew down the length of the North Island, down the length of the South Island, looked at all the mountains, and then flew back up again to Auckland. Just to look! It must have cost tens of thousands of dollars just to look out of the window and see the things he wanted to see. If you have the money you can do almost anything you wish.

Imagine for a moment, that you are woken up one morning by the telephone ringing. On answering it, you discover that you have inherited a huge amount of money. So much money that, if you started spending it flat out every day for the rest of your life, you would never get rid of it. Imagine that. You could buy anything. There would be no limitations. If you had that much money, what would you do?

Would you travel the world? Would you see the world's most beautiful national parks and spend time exploring them? Would you buy an island? What would you put on the island? The most luxurious mansion you can dream of? Would you go shopping? Of course you would! We would *all* go shopping! Imagine you wanted to go to Hawaii but all the tickets were taken, then you could buy the airline itself! Then you could go wherever you like, whenever you like. Perhaps you would stay in the finest hotel in Monaco for a time. It would even be possible to buy the entire hotel. The options and opportunities are almost limitless. If you are wealthy enough you have all the freedom in the world!

One of my dreams was to go to Alaska. Eventually I collected enough air miles to take me there. So, starting at Fairbanks,

I hitchhiked my way down to Anchorage, which took about nine days. A guy took me for a flight in his two-seater Piper Cub, dropping down into forest clearings, flying around looking for moose and grizzly bears. I went salmon fishing with some other guys and there I was standing in the water, catching them one after another. There were grizzly bear footprints in the sand behind me, which was kind of disconcerting!

When you fulfill a dream, you have one less dream. Eventually there will be no dreams left. If you have all the money in the world to do whatever you like, you could easily fulfill your dreams within about five years. But you would get used to it and slowly your perspective would change and life would lose its excitement and fun.

Many years ago I read an article in *Time* magazine written by a psychiatrist to the super-wealthy. He made this statement, *"The despair of the super-wealthy is fathomless."* Isn't that interesting? The super wealthy may have all the freedom of this world but their despair is fathomless. If all of your dreams are fulfilled, then there's nothing more to live for. I have dreams that I know I will never fulfill but I enjoy the dream because the act of dreaming itself makes you alive. If you have no dreams left and there's nothing more you want to do, deadness comes over your soul. Dreams are incredibly important for us. *What this reveals is that the human heart has a capacity to dream of freedoms far beyond what the world has to offer.* This world cannot fulfill your dreams and this world cannot give you the freedom that your heart is designed for. We are not designed for the limited freedom of this world. We are designed for the same freedom that God Himself experiences

WHERE ARE WE HEADING?

The eighth chapter of Romans explains things about Christianity that I had never realized before. It talks of sonship and shows us where God is taking us. Often we only see the benefits of a particular truth but not the basis of its reality. For example, we may think that casting out demons is the purpose of being filled with the Spirit, rather than simply a byproduct of who we are *becoming* in God. Our identity in God is so much greater than the ability to do great things for Him.

From chapter 1 through to chapter 8, Paul is giving an overall picture of God's purposes throughout history, showing how He is working in the world. He finishes this picture with the culmination in the middle of Romans chapter 8. After that, he makes wonderful statements like, *"If God is for us, who can be against us?"* and *"Who can separate us from the love of Christ…Neither height nor depth nor any other thing can separate us from the love of God in Christ Jesus our Lord."* These are wonderful and powerful statements.

I wish to draw your attention back to verse 22, to the statement which says, *"…for we know that the whole creation groans and labors as in the pains of childbirth up until this present time."* As a man, I don't know much about childbirth pains. However, I was with Denise when she was giving birth to Matthew, our youngest son. She went through the whole birth without making a single sound. Nor did she use any kind of painkillers. I was very proud of her but I felt sick watching her, seeing the agony that it was for her. And while she didn't make any sound, she nearly broke every bone in my hand – so I know a little about the pains of childbirth! People tell me that childbirth is a totally absorbing experience. It is impossible to think about anything else when you are giving birth. Paul uses this very metaphor to describe the intensity of God's desire to bring something to birth. The whole of creation is in the pains of childbirth trying to bring forth something! There is an incredible desire in God for His creation to be released from the consequences of the fall and to become free.

God is extremely intentional about what He is doing in our lives. Sometimes we can view our faith as merely an appendage to our lives. We are busy fulfilling many other roles, "I'm an architect, a banker, a policeman, an accountant, a leader in the workplace, a team member, a mother, a father, a mentor, a sportsperson...oh, and I'm also a Christian." But being a Christian means that God is highly intent upon completing a work within you, to make you into something that He has designed. He is working very intentionally. It is not a hobby. This is everything for Him. He is full of purpose about what He is doing.

If we go back to verse 19, there is a beautiful understatement, *"...for the earnest expectation of the creation eagerly waits for the revealing of the sons of God."* God's focus throughout the course of human history is to see His sons and daughters come forth! I believe, as people move more and more deeply into the revelation of God as our Father, experiencing His love and walking with Him in the same kind of relationship that Jesus had, that we are going to see sons and daughters of God rising up, *with an authority far beyond anything that has ever been experienced before.*

This will be a different kind of authority. We have experienced the authority of the Word. We have experienced the authority of the Spirit. We have experienced the authority of ministry gifts. We have experienced the authority of ministry office. But there is a greater authority. The authority of the Father! And it only comes upon sons! When the authority of the Father comes it will be totally infused with love, truth, power, grace, kindness, gentleness, wisdom, and all of His paternal attributes. It is going to be an authority that the world will have absolutely no capacity to withstand. When that authority comes, we are going to see the *sons* and *daughters* of God coming forth out of every nation.

THE AUTHORITY OF SONS AND DAUGHTERS

This is where Christianity is headed. This is the great goal of all creation. When the sons of God are revealed in Christ's likeness we are going to see men and women rising up from every nation with an incredible capacity to speak straight from the Father's heart. Beyond the authority of simply believing the Word, beyond the authority of being filled with the Holy Spirit, but with the authority of the personhood of the Father stamped into their hearts and revealed in His likeness. It says that *"...the whole creation is groaning, waiting to see the revelation of the sons of God."* This is what it is all about!

He is calling us to be sons and daughters appropriate to who He is! Carrying the stamp, the mark, and the *authority* of our Father upon us. The two witnesses in Revelation 11 are a good example of the end result of the purpose of the Father. They tormented the leaders of the world with their preaching and could not be killed with any of the weapons that the world could muster until God allowed it. World leaders are so relieved at their death that they hold a party! But God raises them from the dead in full view of the world and calls them to heaven. I would encourage you to read about them just to get an insight into what the true authority of sonship can actually look like.

When we look at what Paul is saying, that, "...the whole creation is groaning and waiting for the sons of God to be revealed," we see the description of this in verse 21, "...because the creation itself also will be delivered from the bondage of corruption into the glorious freedom of the children of God." The glorious freedom of the children of God! When we look at what it means to be sons and daughters of the Father it shows that He is calling us to be free like He is free.

This is what any good father wants for his child - to have the same level of experience of life that *he* has. We have a Father who is not comparable with a human father but He is the Father from whom every family on the earth is named. In other words, we all get our identity as family and as human beings from the fact that He is our Father. We are part of the family relationship that exists within the Trinity! He is *the* Father, the *real* Father and we are now His real sons and daughters. He has put His spirit into us and He is calling us to come into His love, to experience His fathering until we grow to be sons and daughters appropriate to who *He* is.

There was a movement some years ago called "the manifest sons of God" but it did not have a revelation of the Father. You cannot be a son if you do not have a revelation of the Father. Sonship is not *actually* about sonship. Sonship is about the Father because you are only really a son or daughter when you have a relationship with a father or mother. That is what sonship means. And so, as we are growing in this sonship, He is bringing us into this *glorious freedom* of the children of God.

How free is God?

The kind of freedom that we are called to goes far beyond what we think. When you give your life to the Lord He forgives your sins and you are free. John 8:36 says, "If the Son makes you free, you shall be free indeed." We often relate that to simply being free of sin or being born again, but this freedom goes a long, long way beyond that. That's just the start!

There is a verse in Galatians that I never really understood, not until I started to see this issue of freedom. In Galatians 5:1 it says, *"It is for freedom that Christ has set us free."* I had always wondered about that, because I didn't really know what it meant. Why did Paul repeat the word "freedom" twice? Why didn't he just say, "God has called us to freedom?" He was very deliberate about his use of language because it is *for freedom* that Christ has set us free. I used to think the main reason for being set free was to be released from the bondage of sin. Not so. It is *for freedom* that Christ has set us free. Why? It is because *freedom is our destiny.* He sets us free because freedom is so wonderful, not because bondage is so terrible. He wants us to walk in His freedom and this freedom is an incredible thing.

We dream about this freedom. I believe that our dreams come out of the Garden of Eden, out of the very heart of God. There is an echo of the Garden of Eden within us. Our expectations of how life should treat us in terms of justice and fairness hark back to the Garden of Eden. Despite the injustices that abound in this present world there *is* going to be a day of perfect justice.

We are called to be free like Jesus is free, like the Father is free. But just how free is God? Now here is where it becomes fun.

One thing that I like about Jesus is that He was free of taxes. More accurately put, He paid His taxes, but He was *free of the methods of capitalism to get the money to pay his taxes.* In Matthew 17, Peter went to Jesus with a question. I will paraphrase him, "Lord, the tax man is at the door. Do *we* pay taxes?" Jesus basically replied, "Yes, we do, but we are not limited to the ways of the world." He then told Peter to go fishing, advising him, "When you catch a fish, it is going to have a coin in its mouth and it will be enough for me and for you." It fascinates me that Jesus didn't include the other disciples in this miracle. It was only Peter who asked Jesus and he got to witness the freedom that Jesus operated in. So Jesus was free from the tax systems of this world.

The gifts of the Spirit that Jesus operated in were a demonstration of His freedom from the limitations of human understandings. It wasn't so much that Jesus had a ministry of healing, but rather that He was *free of disease*! He was free of everything from the enemy. He didn't only heal people but He gave them freedom from sickness. He released them from their prison of pain and illness because He walked in this freedom.

He was also *free of the limits of education.* He knew things that didn't come through being taught in a classroom. He was freed into God's perspective of knowledge. The Scripture says that, *"Jesus Christ is made unto us wisdom from God,"* (1 Corinthians 1:30). We can enter into the wisdom of our Father. We can appropriate the knowledge that He has.

Jesus was free of the limitations of our earthly knowledge. He was free from the data that comes through the five senses, through education and learning. He was free from the generally accepted "known" into a knowledge that went far beyond earthly understanding. He walked on water, not because He wanted to walk on water, but because He was free of gravity. Peter wasn't quite as free. He looked at the water and thought, "Arghh! I'm going to sink!" and sink he did until he looked to Jesus to free him from his unbelief. Jesus was free of thinking like that. We see this when He was taken up through the clouds and ascended to His Father. Wouldn't you like to fly? Why do you dream of flying if it is impossible that you ever will?

WE WERE BORN IN A PRISON

Imagine a boy who has been born into a prison without any windows. He grows up in prison, amongst the other prisoners, never knowing that there is anything to life other than the prison. His total perspective of existence is the prison system. He knows nothing else. As time goes on he becomes familiar with all of the systems of the prison and even learns how to use some of them to his advantage in order to gain benefits that the other prisoners don't have. He learns how to manipulate the system because he has become wise about the way the prison operates and about what he can and can't get away with. But everything he does is *still within* the prison. He has never been to the ocean, he has never seen mountains, he doesn't know about farms. In fact, he doesn't know about anything except iron bars, stone walls and the prison regime. He might think he has a good life but we know that he knows little of the real wonders of life.

The point is that each and every one of us *has* been born into a prison. Sir Walter Raleigh made an amazing statement, "The world is nothing but a large prison." It is called "this world," this physical reality, and we think that *this* is all there is to life, that this is the extent of experience. Some of us have become very good at manipulating the systems of this world. We think, "If you can make life better for yourself and you can get a better deal within the world's system, then good for you!" We live our lives believing that this is the best that life has to offer – but it isn't true.

The reality, dear reader, is that we are sons and daughters of God. But when Adam and Eve sinned a veil came down over the human race and obscured the reality of who we are. *We are sons and daughters of Almighty God and He is calling us into His freedom.* He is calling us to look to who our Father is and begin to live a life appropriate to who *He* is. When we begin to live expecting, believing and seeing the supernatural, seeing beyond what we perceive as "real," beyond what is in front of us, beyond the senses, and begin to dream of who we can be in Him, we are beginning to reach out for sonship. The wonderful truth is that God is calling us into something far greater than we realize. The world will try to lock you in. Sometimes even the church will try to lock you into the limitations of working within the system. But we are sons and daughters of Almighty God.

EXPERIENCING THE GLORIOUS FREEDOM

Let me finish by recounting three stories. These stories show how this glorious freedom operates and give us a glimpse into the kind of life that we can expect as sons and daughters appropriate to who our Father is. Two of the stories are from the experiences of friends and one is from my own personal experience.

One of Denise's friends was sitting in her home near Toronto, praying. Suddenly she realized that she was rising off the floor. She went through the roof of her house and out into the night sky. Walls didn't hold Jesus either. She went out into the night sky and began walking through the air, moving at tremendous pace across the Atlantic Ocean, then across Europe. She could see it all passing beneath her. It was as real as any other moment of her life. When she reached Russia, she started descending until she went through the roof of a little house, far away in the backwoods of Siberia. She found herself standing on the kitchen floor behind an old man who was hunched over a table - weeping. She put her hands on his shoulders and began to pray and, as she prayed for him, the joy of the Lord came into his heart.

When he was weeping for joy, she rose up through the roof again, flew to South America, found herself praying for someone else there and then flew back home to her own house. She had never experienced anything like this before. She was so amazed. One day she told Bob Jones the prophet about it and asked, "Bob, what do you think of that?" He said to her, "Well, honey, you're just becoming a real Christian, that's all!"

Another friend from Minneapolis was praying in his bedroom one night when he felt a gust of wind against his face. He opened his eyes to find himself kneeling on a wharf. He had been praying in the early hours of the morning, but there on the wharf it was bright with sunlight. Surprised, he looked around, wondering what was going on. Suddenly he saw a girl further down the wharf screaming and panicking, so he ran down to her and discovered that her friend had fallen into the water and was in difficulty. Neither girl could swim but this guy happened to be a very good swimmer, so he jumped off the wharf and pulled her out of the water. He brought her up onto the wharf and spent a few minutes reassuring the friends. Suddenly he found himself back in his room in Minneapolis, his clothes soaking wet with salt water! He had absolutely no idea where he had been. A few years later he was at a Christian camp when two girls came rushing through the crowd. One was yelling, "You're the man! You're the man who saved me!

The man on the wharf when I fell into the water! Where did you go?" He said to them, "Where *was* that? Where did that happen?" They were incredulous, "You know where it was! You were *there!*" He replied that he had no idea where it had occurred and told them the whole story. They said, "Well, that was in Florida!"

The last story is from my own personal experience. Some years ago we were a family gathering at the home of Denise's mother. It came to the evening and everyone was talking about what to have for dinner. Finally it was decided that we would get pizza, and it was my job to go and pick it up. I went out to the driveway and unlocked the car. Just as I was getting into the car I realized that I had forgotten my wallet. I remembered that it was in the bedroom. But as I was about to go into the house and get it, a quiet little voice somewhere inside me said, "Don't worry about it." I thought, *"Don't worry about it*? I don't have any money on me! There's plenty in my wallet. It's no problem for me to go back and get it. I really need it!" But again came this little voice, "Don't worry about it."

So I shut the car door and started driving towards town - about four miles away. The whole time my mind was thinking, "What am I doing?! I don't know the guy at the pizza place. They're not going to give me a pizza without any money. I should go back and get my wallet!" but somehow my body kept driving the car! I came to a corner where I had to turn right, so I stopped and looked down the road. Nothing coming. I looked the other way – it was clear. And then I noticed, blowing in the wind directly towards me, there was a $10 note. I had never seen money blowing down the road before this and I haven't seen it since. It blew straight towards me and a gust of wind lifted it up over the bonnet of the car. I thought, "I'm going to grab that!" and so I opened the door just as it blew off the bonnet, and came to a stop right on the road beside me. The car

I driving was quite low so I could just pick it up off the ground without even putting my foot outside the car. I closed the door again and went to get the pizza. It came to $9.95! I had plenty of money in my wallet at home, but it was as if the Father was saying, "You think that you are the father of the family but I am just showing you that *I* am your Father." That was a big miracle for me, even though it was a little thing. It made me realize how we are not of this world.

We are the sons and daughters of God. As we learn to walk in the continuous experiencing of Him loving us every day, we will become free. All the things that we uphold as being wonderful, supernatural gifts of God are really just expressions of who we are supposed to be. As the sons and daughters of God are revealed, the kingdom is going to be established and this world is going to change. Everything that has been of Satan will be cast out. The day will be set for the wedding feast of the Lamb and we will all be there. The Father will come and kneel down beside you to wipe away all the tears of pain. The Scripture says, "*Now are we the sons of God. What we shall be is yet to be revealed.*" (1 John 3:2). When we are at the wedding feast we will look at each other and say, "We didn't know the half of it!!!"

We are in the time when the bride is preparing herself for the marriage of the Lamb. We will become the bride of Christ on the wedding day. Traditionally in Jewish marriages the bridegroom doesn't meet his bride until the wedding day. Before that she is being prepared for him. One day we will see Jesus face to face but now we are being prepared for that day.

Abraham (the Father) sent ten camels loaded with gifts from his household with his servant (the Holy Spirit) so that Rebecca would grow accustomed to the love and the family environment that Issac (Jesus) had known all his life. Now it is God the Father who is bestowing upon us all that He is and has, so that we are prepared and made appropriate for marriage to His son.

"NOW WE ARE THE SONS OF GOD."

I feel for the first time in my life that I have really come to understand what the gospel actually is. It is all about a Father who lost His kids and He simply wants them back again. Because the majority of the human race has great difficulty loving authority figures (the fall has caused most people in power to be corrupted by that power) the Father didn't come Himself, but sent His Son to perfectly represent Him and draw us back home to Him.

What an amazing person God is! And we are His sons and daughters! I look forward to the day when we will see sons and daughters in their full expression and freedom, rising up out of every nation of the world, exhibiting and expressing the person, nature and works of our Father, and walking like Jesus in this broken world.

SOURCES

Derek Prince, *Newsletter February 1998*.

C. S. Lewis, *A Grief Observed*, Faber and Faber, London, 1961.

Andrew Murray, *Abiding in Christ*, Bethany House Publishers, Minneapolis, Minnesota, 2003. Originally published in 1895 by Henry Altemus under the title *Abide in Christ*.

Augustine of Hippo as quoted by Fr. Raniero Cantalamessa in *Life in the Lordship of Christ*, Sheed and Ward, Kansas City, 1990.

AN INVITATION...

If you enjoyed reading this book we invite you to a Fatherheart Ministries 'A' School. Fatherheart Ministries 'A' Schools are a one week environment of the revelation of love.

The Two Goals of 'A' Schools are:
1. To give an opportunity for you to have a personal major experience of the love that God the Father has for you.
2. To give the strongest Biblical understanding possible of the place of the Father in the Christian life and walk.

During the school you will be introduced to the full perspective of the revelation of Father's love. Through revelatory insight and sound biblical teaching told through the lives of those that minister you will be exposed to a transforming message of Love, Life and Hope.

You will be given the opportunity to remove the main blockages to receiving Father's love and discover your heart as a true son or daughter. Jesus had the heart of a son to His Father. He lived in the presence of the love of the Father. Johns Gospel tells us that everything that He said and did was what He saw and heard His Father doing. Jesus invites us to enter that world as brothers and sisters of Him the first born.

As we open our hearts Father pours His love into our hearts by the Holy Spirit. In a heart transformed by His love, true and lasting change can occur. After years of striving and perfomance many are finally finding the way home, to a place of rest and belonging.

To apply for an A School visit 'Schools & Events' at
www.fatherheart.net

Additional copies of this book and other resources
from Fatherheart Media are available at:

www.fatherheart.net/shop - New Zealand
www.fatherheartmedia.com - Europe
www.amazon.com - Paperback & Kindle versions

FATHERHEART MEDIA

PO BOX 1039
Taupo, New Zealand 3330

Visit us at www.fatherheart.net

11309244R00111

Printed in Great Britain
by Amazon.co.uk, Ltd.,
Marston Gate.